THE
Retirement Decision

ACHIEVE FINANCIAL INDEPENDENCE WITH YOUR 401(k)

Mike Rose

[signature: Mike Rose]

KAPLAN) PUBLISHING

President, Kaplan Publishing: Roy Lipner
Vice President and Publisher: Maureen McMahon
Senior Acquisitions Editor: Karen Murphy
Production Editor: Karen Goodfriend
Typesetter: the dotted i
Cover Designer: Michael Warrell

Published by Kaplan Publishing,
a division of Kaplan, Inc.

Printed in the United States of America

06 07 08   10 9 8 7 6 5 4 3 2 1

Library of Congress Cataloging-in-Publication Data
Rose, Mike (Michael)
    The retirement decision : achieve financial independence with your 401(k) / Mike Rose.
        p.   cm.
    ISBN-13: 978-1-4195-2695-4
    ISBN-10: 1-4195-2695-2
    1. 401(k) plans. 2. Retirement income—United States—Planning. 3. Investments—United States. I. Title.
    HD7105.45.U6R67 2006
    332.024'0145—dc22
                                                                2006015681

To my lovely wife
Bonnie
and
Soren, Samuel, and Hannah

"Time matters most when decisions are irreversible."[1]

Peter L. Bernstein
Against the Gods

Contents

PART THREE
Invest Wisely

Acknowledgments

I would like to express my sincere gratitude to several people who unselfishly contributed time, encouragement, and expertise to this endeavor.

Peter Flanzer is a long-time colleague and friend from my days in Chicago. Peter believed in this book from the very beginning. He introduced me to Kaplan Publishing and remained committed throughout the stages of its development. His steadfast devotion and reliable counsel were invaluable.

Randi Bowe also lent freely of her advice and encouragement from the book's inception. Her insight and eye for perfection were continually a wonderful resource.

Brian Wang spent long hours reviewing formulas, tables, and various mathematical assumptions. He also offered many helpful suggestions on the manuscript. Brian is a gifted sparring partner.

Special thanks to Warren Buffett for granting permission to include copyrighted material from his Annual Reports. I also want to thank *Outstanding Investor Digest* for permission to include quotations from their many valuable interviews and exceptional reporting, and John Wiley & Sons, Inc. for permission to reuse quotations from Janet Lowe's *Damn Right! Behind the Scenes with Berkshire Hathaway Billionaire Charlie Munger*.

Chris Grant brought intellectual gifts and years of valuable perspective. Jon Flitter, Stephen Allen, and John Akkerman were also willing to share their time; their insight was likewise of great value.

My relationship with Kaplan Publishing has been a pleasure. They have been a tremendous partner in the writing, editing, and publishing of this book. Since the beginning, their responsiveness and support have been critical to the manuscript's completion. Special thanks to Karen Murphy, Mary Good, Eileen Johnson, Karen Goodfriend, Maureen McMahon, Roy Lipner, and the entire publishing team who have simply been outstanding.

My wife, Bonnie, has been tireless in her dedication to this book and to me. Our two sons and daughter, Soren, Sam, and Hannah, have also done much to both support and inspire this effort. I wish finally to acknowledge my parents, Ann and the late Dave Rose, for providing a childhood where hard work and thrift were valued, and thinking independently was expected.

Introduction

This book was written for people who think seriously about their retirement. It is for people who are concerned, if not a bit anxious, about having enough money put away for their final years; individuals who have many thoughtful questions about their financial futures and who are genuinely seeking legitimate answers. The book is for workers who someday hope to pursue interests that lie beyond their employment with a certain sense of serenity, security, and independence. It was written for those who very much want to be on the right track with their saving and investing.

401(k) retirement plans first emerged around 1982. The oldest baby boomer was 36 years old; the youngest was still in high school. The Dow Jones Industrial Average spent much of that year below 1000. Bonds paid fixed rates of interest above 10 percent—guaranteed by the full faith and credit of the U.S. government. It was a wonderful time for the introduction of a radically new way to save and invest for retirement. The idea was named after section 401(k), of the Internal Revenue Service (IRS) code.

Companies sponsor 401(k) plans for the benefit of employees. Those who elect to participate can currently save up to $15,000 annually, or $20,000 for those 50 years of age or older. The contributions, which come from your paycheck, are generally tax deductible, which means the IRS treats your deferrals much like the interest on mortgage payments. All of your earnings, interest, and dividends grow tax deferred until you either retire or withdraw the money.[1] In my judgment, 401(k) plans are near-perfect vehicles for the creation of individual wealth.

Those who are depending on their 401(k) to provide the bulk of their income at retirement will find this book most helpful. You, in other words, comprise the target audience if you are counting on your 401(k) plan to be the train pulling most of the freight when it comes to retirement. To that end, a great many of you are genuinely thrilled to be able to participate in a 401(k) at work. Some of you are in a 401(k) plan because somewhere along the line a decision was made to terminate your traditional pension plan. Others are participating in a 401(k) plan because it was either that or nothing. A few of you may not even know what type of retirement plan you have at work—or if you are even covered under a plan at all.

Most of you have little or no say over the investment choices offered in your 401(k). Some of you have more than 50 different investment options while others may only have three or four selections. The investment vehicles of choice in most 401(k) plans are index funds, mutual funds, or annuity products. Many of you understand the investment options made available to you and are quite pleased with the choices. Some of you are no doubt frustrated and displeased with the choices. A few, I would guess, don't spend much time thinking about it one way or the other.

There are many 401(k) plans that offer generous employer-matching contributions. This means that when you participate in the plan by saving from each paycheck, the company "matches" your contribution with additional money. Some plans do not offer matching dollars.

A few of you would like to save more in your 401(k), but are limited because of certain IRS regulations. About half of you work for companies that spend a great deal of time educating employees on the retirement plans. Other companies are less visibly engaged with employee retirement education.

Interestingly, and importantly, the 401(k) issues just referenced that are completely beyond your control will ultimately have very little effect on whether you achieve your retirement goals. The playing field, at least in this regard, is level and generally fair regardless of where you live and work in America. Certainly, superior investment options, generous company matching contributions, and attention to educational matters will give workers a definite advantage as they pursue retirement objectives, but these are merely secondary considerations to the process of wealth creation.

You, as an individual, and the decisions you make as an individual over your working lifetime, are what control the process of personal wealth creation within your 401(k) plan. Having enough money put away for your retirement is largely a self-controlled process. You are the person making the critically important decisions. You call the shots. You own the process. It is your show. Becoming wealthy, in other words, is your decision. For example, there are all kinds of ways companies can improve their 401(k) plans—they can upgrade the investment choices, negotiate lower fees, increase the matching contribution, and expand the participant education program—but none of these enhancements can make you financially independent by retirement age. Only you can make the retirement decision.

Those who reflect seriously about the connection between wealth and their 401(k) at work understand there are five questions that must be legitimately answered:

1. How much money will I need to retire?
2. How can I measure the progress I've made already with saving and investing to see if I'm ahead or behind in my efforts?
3. How much money should I be saving each pay period to reach my retirement goal?
4. If I am in my 40s and 50s, and behind in my savings, how can I put a plan in place to catch up?
5. Can I handle a stock market crash? Am I in the right investments?

As you have probably already realized, it is going to be extremely difficult to reach your retirement goal without the answers to these five very basic questions. The message of this book is one that is straightforward and easy to understand. It is the story of how everyday people can achieve their financial targets by retirement age. Each of these five basic questions, as well as many others, are addressed and answered specifically for you within the pages that follow. Time will be devoted to studying some of the greatest investors ever, but the book will focus mostly on you and what you must do to reach your goal by retirement age.

It has taken nearly 20 years to think through some of the answers to these five questions. These questions, although basic, are not easy ones to answer. Thus, I think it is important for you to know that I have spent the better part of a professional lifetime working closely with companies that sponsor 401(k) plans and alongside the workers who participate in these unique retirement programs. The workplace provided the classroom wherein these five questions originated and where many of the answers were discovered. This is not a book about theoretical or philosophical diversions, but rather the practical application of saving and investing.

This book is written as a narrative. The stories in each chapter convey important lessons on wealth creation. The content in each chapter builds on the chapter before until one last question is answered in Chapter 15. Skipping ahead to read those chapters or passages of particular interest will likely be less meaningful without first reading the preceding stories. Those who spend the time necessary to read the book in its entirety will profit most.

Finally, an important word about some of the people you will read about in this book. When I began this study on wealth creation, I started with Warren Buffett, who is arguably the greatest investor ever. It soon became apparent, however, that one cannot fully understand Buffett without also studying his longtime business partner, Charlie Munger. And one cannot grasp Munger without reading Benjamin Franklin and Daniel Defoe. Great care has been taken to ensure that Buffett and Munger's quotations remain within their proper context. Please do not conclude that either Warren Buffett or Charlie Munger have personally endorsed any of the views put forth by me. Hopefully, after reading this book, you'll be inspired to read more about these two great men. You're sure to wind up personally enriched by investing meaningful time contemplating their observations and thoughts.

A good book will stay in your mind for as long as 20 or 30 years and continue to challenge your thinking and inspire your impressions. It takes the better part of a generation to become wealthy. For most, it is a journey with all sorts of twists and turns—long, dry stretches and times of unbelievably good fortune. Seasoned travelers, before embarking on any significant trip, tend to pick their companions carefully. The words that follow lend guidance and will steady the many ups and downs that surely lie ahead on the road to wealth. It is a book that takes you to your goal and returns you home again, safely.

Mike Rose
Summit, NJ

PART ONE

Three Constants of Wealth Creation

The Reckoning

It's fine to have a blowout in a fancy restaurant,
With terrapin and canvas back and all the wine you want;
To enjoy the flower and music, watch the pretty women pass
Smoke a cigar, and sip the wealthy water in your glass.
It's bully in a high tones joint to eat and drink your fill,
But it's quite another matter when you

Pay the bill.

It's great to go out every night on fun or pleasure bent;
To wear your glad rags always and to never save a cent;
To drift along regardless, have a good time every trip;
To hit the high spots sometimes, and to let your chances slip;
To know you're acting foolish, yet go on fooling still,
Till nature calls a showdown, and you

Pay the bill.

Time has got a little bill get wise while yet you may,
For the debit side's increasing in a most alarming way;
The things you had no right to do, the things you should have done,
They're all put down; it's up to you to pay for every one.
So eat, drink, and be merry, have a good time if you will,
But God help you when the time comes, and you

Foot the bill.[1]

Robert Service

CHAPTER 1

The Reckoning

A couple of summers ago my family and I were driving across the pristine wilderness of the Yukon Territory. At day's end we secured lodging for the evening in an old log cabin. We then made our way across the road and settled down for some supper at a small café. Sitting next to us were two men. They were talking loudly. Neither, it seemed, knew the other. They had met just a little while earlier while also traveling through the great Yukon. Both were motorcycle enthusiasts, and both were traveling the Alaskan Highway all the way from Dawson's Creek, British Columbia, to Fairbanks, Alaska. It had been a long day for both of them on the endless two-lane road. It was apparent that the men, each somewhere between 50 and 60 years of age, shared a common interest in adventure, solitude, and speed. They were drinking beer, laughing, and telling tall tales about what, to almost any man, was one of the greatest life experiences one could ever imagine: riding a Honda Golden Wing through the Alaskan and Yukon wilderness.

Dinner was eventually finished. Before parting, however, one man asked the other a question. "I assume," he said to the other, "you are able to travel so much on your motorcycle because you're independently wealthy?" Their spirited conversation suddenly grew ominously quiet. The other man calmly lowered his nearly empty mug on the table and pondered the question for a few seconds. "No," the man responded softly, "I am not wealthy. I do own a small business. I am a self-employed auto mechanic. And my wife is a scientist. She obviously is a big supporter of my cycling hobby."

The first man spoke again. "You know something, the other day I calculated what my 401(k) account and Social Security would pay each month in retirement. I just couldn't believe it. I used to think all I was ever going to do in retirement was just ride motorcycles. The truth is, in retirement I'm not even going to be able to afford a motorcycle."

Listening, the other man took his final swig of beer. "I know exactly what you mean. The reason I'm up here in the Yukon is I wanted to make sure I could complete this trip while there is still money available. There is no way I'll be able to afford this in retirement."

Peter Thiel, a professional money manager, observed that today people are borrowing more and saving less. "What makes that not just extreme, but insane," states Thiel, "is that we're talking about 40-something and 50-something baby boomers who should be saving like crazy for retirement. People are spending as though they will get a heart attack and die on the day they turn 65. People will reach 65 with a big house and no savings and have to work until they're 85."[2]

It doesn't require too much savvy to understand that the retirement landscape in America is shifting rapidly. Unless hard-working Americans comprehend fully what they must do to successfully navigate through the uncertain shoals of financial independence, the outcome on an individual basis will likely be disappointing. Insufficient savings in retirement will require change in one's standard of living. And all the alternatives surrounding this change in one's standard of living are bad. It is much like picking poison.

The two 50-something motorcyclists, meeting by chance in the Yukon, understood well this unfortunate prescription for change. They knew that unpleasant decisions were just around the bend, because neither had accumulated money enough to support their standard of living in retirement. The motorcycles would have to go. And the motorcycles were probably just the tip of the iceberg. Who knows what other amenities would follow those motorcycles out the door?

A common story beginning to unfold in America is the very real prospect of millions and millions of workers nearing retirement age with insufficient savings. Insufficient savings is gentle wording. A great many are approaching retirement with literally nothing put away. Nothing!

People who have worked hard their entire lives. People who have made sacrifices to raise good families and provide the best of everything for their children. People who have paid for college educations; paid for trips to Disney World; paid for visits to the orthodontist; and spent lavishly on new cars, new clothes, new furniture, new televisions, and new appliances—which have led to the overstuffing of already oversized houses—will soon find themselves, perhaps for the first time ever, unable to "foot the bill."

The facts, by some accounts, are unbelievably dismal. In the United States, among households whose heads are aged 55 to 59, a full 36 percent have zero account balances in their individual retirement accounts (IRAs) or defined contribution retirement plans at work. In other words, almost 4 out of every 10 of these households, between the ages of 55 and 60, have nothing put away for retirement. The median retirement savings account for Americans aged 55 to 59 is a paltry $10,400 per household. Even those in this age group who have tried to plan and save for retirement, have little more than $50,000 on balance in their retirement accounts.[3] "The retirement savings shortfall is not just extreme," according to Peter Thiel, "but insane."

There is no reason for any working American to approach retirement with insufficient savings. To believe otherwise is subscription to a myth. Quite simply, there are no excuses for any working American to spend more than 80,000 hours at work collecting an average of 1,000 paychecks over a 40-year time period, and not have something put away. Only in extreme cases of illness, injury, or incapacity can one possibly justify "blowing" nearly 1,000 paychecks!

The two Yukon motorcyclists fit the retirement savings shortfall perfectly. These men were successful throughout their professional careers. The men were handsome, articulate, intelligent, humorous, and considerate. Neither appeared irresponsible.

Despite their strong bearing and accomplishments, these men did not escape the demographics of their age group: the $50,000 retirement savings account. These two men somehow got themselves trapped, along with so many other millions of 50-somethings who are now discovering their retirement savings to be insufficient. Soon, unless 50-something workers take charge of their savings and begin the process of increasing the balances within their retirement accounts, many difficult choices will be made. It is reminiscent of the early pioneers and their Conestoga wagons. When the trails grew high and steep, and the rivers wide and deep, treasured heirlooms not essential for survival were left behind. In retirement, those unable to support their current standard of living will also decide what treasured life choices get left behind.

The chances are good these men were never told early in life just how much money it takes to maintain a decent lifestyle in retirement. The chances are even better that no one ever told them how much to set aside for retirement savings each pay period. No one ever sat these men down when they were young and had them calculate the total number of hours they would work and estimate the paychecks they would collect. No one explained to them how just modest sums saved in the early years compound into unbelievably huge amounts of money over time. It is doubtful anyone ever offered advice that was both impartial and sound on how credible investment vehicles are identified. Because these men were otherwise successful in their education and professions, it was perhaps just assumed somewhere along the line they would finish their careers with a surfeit of savings. The truth of the matter is that these guys, like so many of their contemporaries, had basically no understanding of how individual wealth is created. Awareness of their future financial condition came just a little late.

A hundred years before these two motorcyclists met by chance in the Yukon, there lived in the same northern wilderness a poet named Robert Service. His poems, one of which opens this chapter, embraced the rugged individualism of those who were drawn to the frozen Canadian frontier by the lure of gold. Service spent 16 long years in the Yukon wilderness with men who had forfeited everything in the hope of striking it rich. His observations on the human condition underscore a piercing insight into the triumphs and failures of individual character that so often define life and death.

When the news of the Klondike gold strike reached Seattle in the spring of 1898, approximately 100,000 men and women dropped everything and began the treacherous expedition north into the Alaskan and Yukon wilderness. The mountainous terrain forced many to literally crawl on their hands and knees for miles up cragged passages facing headlong into winds of 60 miles per hour, in temperatures of –65°F. A full 60,000 either dropped out or died along the way; 40,000 eventually survived the horrid journey only to discover that most of the stakes had already been claimed. Sadly, only 4 out of every 1,000 people who began the trip ever returned home with a fortune.[4] Most financial manias, like the Yukon gold rush, are finished by the time crowds appear. The probability of getting rich quick is seldom, if ever, favorable.

It is one of the great ironies of human nature that people are inclined to sacrifice nearly everything when the odds of making it rich are near zero and will hardly sacrifice a thing when the probability of becoming wealthy is close to certainty. As we've just seen, the atmosphere surrounding the Klondike gold rush was electric. When the news of the gold rush first hit Seattle, thousands of people, including the mayor, immediately dropped everything and headed north. Another incredible example is seen prior to the great stock market crash of 1929, when many investors had borrowed against their net worth by a ratio of nine times, and put it all in the market, before getting wiped out for good. Again, in the early 1970s, a basket of stocks named the "Nifty Fifty" soared and then dropped without warning, thus destroying the fortunes of both professional and amateur investors. Yet again, the 20th century finally closed with the investing public in a whirlwind of euphoria over Internet and telecommunication and technology stocks. Investment bankers and mutual fund companies could hardly manufacture shares fast enough to satisfy speculative demand before the infamous Internet bubble popped and trillions of dollars disappeared. It is indeed astonishing to witness the sacrifices people will make in the pursuit of getting rich whenever they think a short cut has been discovered.

The Meaning of Wealth

Wealth is defined by financial independence. Those who are financially independent, or wealthy, can live for the remainder of their days without compromising their standard of living or running out of money. They have accumulated enough assets to maintain their prescribed lifestyles indefinitely. The wealthy do not depend on receiving a paycheck to make ends meet.

The words *wealthy* and *financially independent* will be used synonymously throughout this book. The word *rich* will be used sparingly. There is a difference between the wealthy and the rich. The rich, as Ernest Hemingway once noted, have more money. The rich, in fact, have an overabundance of money. Bill Gates, the founder of Microsoft, is rich.

He could spend a $1 million a day for the next 100 years and still not exhaust his fortune. Few ever become rich, whereas nearly all working Americans can become wealthy.

Individuals have been confounded since the beginning of time over the mystery of wealth creation. Despite the prosperity of Western civilization and the unbridled growth of America since 1800, the great majority of workers are at a complete loss whenever it comes to articulating basic principles of wealth creation. The conundrum of money growth sweeps across the wide spectrum of socioeconomic and class lines. The executive in the corner suite is often no more knowledgeable about how wealth is created than the worker on the line. The mystery of wealth and wealth creation is pervasive throughout the workforce.

I remember well a friendly conversation that took place once with a physician. She was curious as to whether I had ever been to a casino. I replied that I had not. The physician was incredulous.

"You mean to tell me you have never once been to a casino?"

"Never."

The physician appeared momentarily surprised. "Well, I went to a casino once when I was in school," she said. "It is really something to see. You ought to visit one sometime. It is a great place to study people."

I politely chuckled. "I have no interest in studying those people. Their story has already been studied and the odds makers have their number. I want to study people who have started from scratch and become wealthy over time."

"Oh, come on," she cajoled. "You don't really believe people can become wealthy without getting lucky do you?"

The thought of any typical worker becoming independent financially appears inconceivable to many. That is why the physician so fervently believed that personal wealth, for most people, hinges upon a lucky break or a lifetime of favorable breaks. Although good luck can, under certain conditions, accelerate the normal timetable for financial independence, personal wealth creation seldom depends on luck. Luck, in fact, runs counter to the individual process of wealth creation. Luck is a statistical aberration. Luck is the unexpected rare event that is unrepeatable. Luck is winning a round of bingo or hitting a hole-in-one. Luck, as a rule, is the sole consequence of external factors that lie beyond one's control. The accumulation of wealth over a working lifetime is a self-controlled process. Individuals who start from nothing and become independently wealthy make choices in life that shape their financial destiny.

Remarkably, most working Americans can become financially independent within a time span of 30 to 40 years. Lower-paid workers are just as able to become wealthy over time as higher-paid workers. External factors such as annual income, occupation, social standing, or even luck have little to do with personal wealth creation. It is, however, understood that the process of wealth creation is more difficult for lower-income workers. The sacrifices are obviously more demanding for those who earn less. Personal wealth, nonetheless, is largely predicated on internal considerations and convictions controlled by the self, such as sacrifice, initiative, forethought, and fidelity. Wealth creation, in other words, depends on an individual's determination.

There are 45 million Americans covered under company-sponsored 401(k) plans at this time. These workers are diligently saving and investing for their anticipated retirements as the country quietly moves away from the old world of comprehensive government guardianship and corporate paternalism to a more recent notion of "ownership society." Responsibility for financial security in retirement, in other words, is shifting subtly away from the collective and toward the individual. The ultimate impact of this change affects not just those who participate in 401(k) plans, but in a larger sense, all who work in America.

This impending "ownership society," like any new frontier, is rife with meaningful opportunities as well as pronounced risks. Redistributing wealth back to the individual will unquestionably produce mixed results. Some workers will very likely experience much prosperity, while others run the real risk of getting left behind as they encounter unforeseen hazards along the way. One fact, however, appears indisputably certain: Workers need to know whether they are behind the curve, ahead of the curve, or on track. Problems do indeed brew solutions. Those, however, who are completely oblivious to the possibility of problems are likely to someday encounter not just great hardship, but irreparable harm. Workers no longer have the luxury of flying blind whenever it comes to financial matters.

Ownership Is the Product of Optimism

The first monthly Social Security check was issued to Ida Mae Fuller in 1940. Three years earlier, when taking the oath of office for a second time, President Franklin D. Roosevelt observed that one-third of the nation was "ill-housed, ill-clad, and ill-nourished." The national economy was near ruin. People were desperate. The average American family in 1937 was living on less than $3.75 a day. It was virtually impossible for average families to own their homes. Most rented apartments and houses.[5]

Social Security was a much needed government insurance program in 1940. This single piece of legislation spared millions and millions of Americans the dreadful consequences of being forgotten and indigent in old age. The elderly covered under Social Security have never had to worry about receiving their monthly checks from the government. The pledge to protect the dignity of older citizens has rightfully been inviolate ever since the final years of the Great Depression.

Fortunately, the economic climate has improved immeasurably since Roosevelt's second term. Abject poverty, which once was pervasive in the 1930s, has been replaced by a remarkable sense of optimism and prosperity. Higher education and training are available for most Americans, jobs are plentiful, and uninterrupted streams of technological advances continue to open new opportunities for human innovation and capital. Hunger, cold, and insufficient clothing are practically foreign to most who live in America.

Ownership is the product of optimism. Whenever people are confident, prosperity flourishes. America's emergence from the Great Depression was marked by an astounding increase in home ownership. Today, in contrast to the 1930s, the great majority of average American families own their homes. In fact, 9 percent of Americans own a second home. Bankers, once made confident of the Depression's demise, were eager to loan money. Families, optimistic of their prospects, were willing to mortgage a significant slice of their wages for the title to a lot and house. Home ownership brings stability and independence to families. Homes anchor existence. Americans, like nearly all people across the globe, are most secure whenever they are able to experience ownership.

Interestingly, the shift to an "ownership society" is in many respects grounded in the G.I. Bill of Rights. Following the Great Depression and World War II, the government implemented a special program for returning veterans whereby those who served received assistance with college tuition. By "the late forties, veterans would constitute almost 50 percent of the male students in all institutions of higher learning."[6] The G.I. program did much to transform American society as millions of newly minted engineers, teachers, physicians, and other highly-skilled professionals expanded the U.S. workforce. Individuals, when given the opportunity to invest in themselves, built a society that was far different from pre-war America. America's standard of living, following World War II, soon became the envy of the entire world as roots to a new "ownership society" began to take hold. The purpose, likewise, of a 401(k) retirement plan is to offer workers this same opportunity to invest in themselves by saving toward the goal of becoming wealthy at retirement.

Ownership, in other words, is fundamental to personal stability. This was one of the most unforgettable lessons of the Great Depression. Those without the means to "ownership" were frequently humiliated and repressed. Landlords, after all, call the shots. They pick the wallpaper, decide the fate of pets, and fix the furnace on their timetable. Landlords make and enforce the rules to protect their own interests. Worse yet, landlords can sell a house from under tenants whenever circumstances and price are right. Those who do not "own" often forfeit serenity and dignity.

An ownership society encourages people to take control of and embrace their financial destiny. One objective of an ownership society is for each working American to someday become wealthy or financially secure. Social Security was a precious lifeline for those who suffered during the Great Depression. Few things, however, change perspective like time. Social Security, despite a long and honorable history of successfully providing monthly income to older Americans, still operates in principle much like a Depression-era landlord. The government "owns" the assets. Special interest groups and politicians create and enforce the rules. Worse yet, there are virtually no guarantees. Future benefits can be altered and even eliminated. Social Security, unlike the G.I. Bill, 401(k) plans, and IRAs, does not build individual wealth. Social Security instead transfers wealth from workers to retirees. The question is not whether Social Security is broken and in need of repair. Social Security, for the record, is likely to survive just fine. The question is whether workers can ever experience legitimate financial security when the landlord is calling the shots. The opportunity to pursue personal financial independence is perhaps best understood as being every bit as much a part of the American dream as home ownership.

This book begins with the belief that most workers have fallen behind in their retirement savings. The shifting retirement landscape has done much to sandwich middle-aged Americans between the diminishing benefits of generations before them and the new expectations of those generations who follow. Yet the plight of these middle-aged Americans is by no means desperate. Middle-aged Americans, as we shall learn later, can harness resources to prevail over retirement savings shortfalls.

There are basically just three problems in life that prevent workers from retiring wealthy:

1. People don't believe they can become wealthy.
2. People don't save enough to become wealthy.
3. People don't invest wisely enough to become wealthy.

Common to all three problems is the word *don't*. "Don't," when used within this context, represents a lack of will or action or direction. Removing "don't" from each problem produces a solution. The creation of personal wealth, as this book will explain, originates from within an individual. Wealth, as mentioned earlier, is a self-controlled process. Wealth is not necessarily determined by high-paying jobs, spectacular investment returns, good luck, or other external factors that are typically beyond the ordinary worker's control. The road to wealth is made manifest by those workers who welcome the opportunity to shape their own destinies.

The ancient Greeks devised a term called *enchiridion*, which means, "ready at hand." An enchiridion was a kind of "handbook for the busy person." It was similar to an executive summary or abridged training manual. It usually was a small book containing the vital details to an important subject.[7]

Looking back, such a handbook on financial independence would have been invaluable for my wife and me, when first saving for retirement: a road map, or *pasó por aquí*, written by someone who had already "passed through here"; a manual on wealth creation outlining and identifying some of the invariable "ups" and "downs" of saving and investing over a working lifetime; an enchiridion that would have been read cover to cover, time and time again.

This book is the culmination of spending 20 years observing individual workers from all stations of life trying to become financially secure. This book does not piggyback on any established product or methodology or market. It gleans from the valuable experiences and writings of many who have skillfully navigated their way to personal wealth creation. Their common stories of success lay the foundation for the process of personal wealth creation.

Thomas Jefferson, author of the Declaration of Independence, was an avid reader. Some scholars have even hinted that Jefferson was obsessed with books. He approached each volume, wrote one biographer, "as though it contained a revelation."[8] Indeed, it is true: Most people who invest time to seriously read books look either for instruction or validation. The primary objective of this book is to unveil the mystery of personal wealth creation. Those who read for instruction will learn how ordinary individuals attain financial independence. The book will explain how money grows and discuss common mistakes to avoid when pursuing financial goals. Those who seek validation will discover exactly where they are on the road to wealth and what they must continue doing to become financially independent.

CHAPTER 2

The Oracle

I think when you're trying to teach the great concepts that work, it helps to tie them into the lives and personalities of the people who developed them.[1]
Charlie Munger, Vice Chairman, Berkshire Hathaway

Each year, around the first or second week in May, thousands of investors converge upon the city of Omaha, Nebraska. The Quest Center fills with upwards of 19,000 people, who all have made the pilgrimage to Omaha at their own expense in order to attend the Berkshire Hathaway annual shareholders' meeting. Journalists from around the globe cover this annual gathering. Investors want to know what Warren Buffett, chairman of Berkshire Hathaway, and Charlie Munger, vice chairman, are thinking. People want to see these two men in person. They want to listen to and ask questions of two of the world's greatest investors.

Likewise, in the ancient world, people traveled at their own expense from all over Greece and beyond to have their questions about the future answered by the Oracle at Delphi. According to legend, the Greek god Apollo spoke through these oracles, who were generally believed to be older women with impeccable reputations. Pilgrims traveled to a sacred temple in Delphi where the oracles resided. Here the oracles offered counsel on a wide variety of subjects, ranging from mathematics to politics. The oracles' predictive powers, however, were the big draw at Delphi. Backed by the credibility of Apollo, individuals hoping to shortcut the future, willingly offered up tremendous financial sacrifices to the oracles for what they hoped would be a glimpse into time.

Warren Buffett is known affectionately as the Oracle of Omaha. Although he lacks the credibility of being an ancient god, he is one of the very few humans alive to ever have taken a dollar and made it grow 60,000 times in value. This contrasts with the average growth of a dollar over a working lifetime of 45 years, which is around 24 times. Henry Emerson, one of the many who faithfully attend the annual Berkshire Hathaway meeting, encapsulates Buffett's incredible investment success in the following scenario:

> Anyone investing $10,000 in *Buffett Partnership, Ltd.* at its inception in 1956 who reinvested the proceeds into Berkshire Hathaway at the partnership's termination in 1969 would today own shares worth over $340 million. And that's after all the taxes, fees, and expenses. Just in case that's not sufficiently mind numbing for you, consider that before fees, but after taxes, the value would've been closer to $600 million.[2]

Buffett's investment acumen has made him rich beyond belief. It is largely for this reason the masses descend on Omaha each year. People want to divine the secret for becoming rich.

Sitting next to Warren Buffett each year at the Berkshire annual meeting is Buffett's longtime friend, business partner, and fellow billionaire, Charlie Munger. Many do not realize the tremendous impact Charlie Munger has had on Berkshire's rich history because Buffett's affiliation with Berkshire Hathaway has been so pronounced. Charlie Munger, in short, is the voice that has complemented the Oracle of Omaha for more than 30 years. It was through Charlie Munger that Warren Buffett was able to forge a consensus on many of the utterly brilliant investment decisions made on behalf of Berkshire Hathaway shareholders. Howard Buffett, the eldest son of Buffett, even says that his father is the second smartest man he knows—Charlie Munger is the first.[3] Warren Buffett, himself, once wrote this about his boon companion, Charlie Munger:

> He is generous in the deepest sense and never lets ego interfere with rationality. Unlike most individuals who hunger for the world's approval, Charlie judges himself entirely by an inner scorecard—and he is a tough grader.[4]

Together, Buffett and Munger open the floor for questions at the annual Berkshire Hathaway meeting. The two men then patiently address inquiries from the audience, usually for hours at a time. But Buffett and Munger do not whisper stock tips into the microphone or make bold predictions concerning the stock market. These seasoned billionaires know that neither market predictions nor hot tips make people wealthy over time. They know people become wealthy when they first identify and then subscribe to the tasks essential for the growth of personal money.

Anyone, then, starting out with the intent of someday becoming wealthy would be wise to initiate this journey with Warren Buffett. He and Charlie Munger are perfect role models. Both started basically from the means of middle-class America. Neither was born rich. One, in fact, suffered a series of missteps and setbacks and was nearly broke by the age of 30. Buffett and Munger grew wealthy by the book. They are honest, patient, disciplined, and industrious. Their word is good. Both, also significantly, came from families where integrity was revered. People, maintained Charlie Munger, were not afraid to give Warren Buffett money because they knew the Buffett family name. The Buffett name, as well as Munger's, has always been synonymous with "honorable" in the city of Omaha. Their lives demonstrate clearly that future personal outcomes, such as starting from modest means and becoming wealthy, are generally predictable and favorable whenever one follows the right path in life.

The 2001 Berkshire shareholder meeting in Omaha was much like many of the other annual gatherings. Buffett and Munger were on stage and behind the microphones fielding questions and offering observations on a wide variety of subjects. Interestingly, a 10-year-old boy rose from his seat and made his way to a microphone. The boy stood in front of the more than 10,000 people and asked two of the world's richest men the following question. "In school, they don't teach you how to make and save money—not in high school or college. So my question is, how would you propose to educate kids in this area?" Buffett replied, "That is a good question. . . . What it takes really—and you find it in some schools and you don't in others—are teachers who can explain the subject. Charlie will say that Ben Franklin was the best teacher of all in that respect."[5]

A little 10-year-old asked a very profound question at the 2001 Berkshire Hathaway annual shareholders meeting! However, it is not just kids who need to know. There are millions of adults in the workplace with this same concern: The mechanic, the nurse, the salesperson, the pilot, the engineer, the biochemist, the plumber, the attorney, the landscaper, the waiter, the physician, the teacher, the banker, the administrative assistant. How does one save and grow money? Schools teach accounting, finance, business management, and security analysis, but curriculums devoted to personal wealth creation for young people as well as the mainstream worker are basically nonexistent.

Prevalent among the great majority of workers who invest and save for retirement are three universal sets of questions:

1. Will I have enough money at retirement or should I save more? Will I be financially independent?
2. How much money should someone my age, with my income, have put away already? Am I ahead or behind the curve? Am I saving enough?
3. Am I in the right investments or should I be doing something else? Would a market crash wipe me out? Do I have too much money in stocks?

Few people anywhere who participate in company-sponsored 401(k) plans can answer these basic questions. Further, no advantage falls to those with impressive titles or elevated salaries. Managers and those working on the line all face the same dilemma. The path to financial independence eludes most who comprise the modern workforce.

The Roman Rule

Ralph Waldo Emerson lived in the early 1800s and is considered by many historians to be one of America's first philosophers. Whenever he appeared to give a speech or publicly read from his writings and essays, great crowds would appear. He was one of the most popular and widely known Americans in the early days of our nation.

Times, obviously, were much different back then, especially when it came to public entertainment. Politics, for instance, was great popular entertainment. Elections were very competitive, and the political landscape surrounding voters was just brutal. Americans in the early 19th century also had a pronounced passion for learning. New ideas and new philosophies were openly embraced in this young country. A smart guy like Emerson, who challenged conventional thought and the status quo, was warmly embraced whenever he toured the country and spoke. He was adored by the crowds, much like rock stars are today. America in the early 1800s was a brand-new country. People fresh to our shores were enthusiastic about getting a clean start. Many wanted to know how they could make the most of this wonderful and great opportunity. There was a premium on learning.

Ralph Waldo Emerson may have presented a nearly perfect model for learning how to become wealthy. Writing in his journal on the last day of August 1839, Emerson recalled that it was "the Roman rule to teach a boy nothing that he could not learn standing."[6] One learns, inferred Emerson, by doing. Education works best when it is active, vibrant, and engaged. An important key to becoming wealthy is to study the great masters and then emulate their ways. Observing and doing, or what Emerson referred to as a Roman education, is the preference for becoming wealthy.

Observe closely, then, the lives of Warren Buffett, Charlie Munger, and Benjamin Franklin (all of who became financially independent rather early in their lives) and you can uncover valuable insight on becoming wealthy. Surely, there are no greater masters at personal wealth creation than these three men. Their path through life is a kind of instructional legacy. You can learn to become wealthy, in other words, by learning to do what these men have practiced. It is the Roman rule.

When studying these wealth builders to learn about what makes them exceptional at what they do, it is helpful to discover constants among them. Constants, for our purposes, are characteristics or principles common to Buffett, Munger, and Franklin that can be adopted by anyone and still produce the same result. What, in other words, does Warren Buffett practice that I can observe and do also to become wealthy? Further, constants are not bound by time or space. For example, take the matter of time. If Benjamin Franklin employed a certain principle 275 years ago when becoming wealthy as a young man, then that same principle should also work today, as well as 275 years from now, provided the principle is a constant. It is the same with space. If Charlie Munger is doing something to build personal wealth in southern California that is a constant, then someone in China, India, England, or Russia ought to be able to emulate this same constant with similar results. Constants, then, are universal practices that, when copied by any other person, will produce similar results regardless of when (time) or where (space) these traits are emulated. The discovery of constants enables one to begin building an educational model for the creation of personal wealth.

Looking at one notable example from the past helps one realize the incredible significance of constants. A little over 100 years ago, Albert Einstein forever changed humanity's understanding of the universe with the discovery of a constant: the speed of light. The speed of light, observed Einstein, never changes. Einstein, a lowly clerk in a Swiss patent office, published his radical conclusions in a paper on special relativity. His work dramatically revolutionized humanity's perception of the known universe. His findings were so extreme many considered them bizarre. He claimed that time is relative (the slower one travels the faster a person's watch ticks). Also, he noted that space bends or is capable of warping. A great many scientists were reluctant to embrace Einstein's counterintuitive conclusions. There was just one problem with conventional thought: Einstein had his facts straight. Einstein, as a result of his work with light, taught the world a powerful lesson on the significance of identifying constants.

We next shall study briefly the early years of Warren Buffett, Charlie Munger, and Benjamin Franklin. Surprisingly, the final outcome of their lives is not what made these three men great. Rather it was certain ideas, beliefs, and character traits that were adopted in their formative years that led to such tremendous wealth and fame in their later years. What, for example, distinguished these men from their peers? What, in their approach to work and saving, was constant in all three men and made the difference between their outcomes and those of their contemporaries? Were their actions repeatable, or were they just lucky? And what are the constants, among these giants, that can be passed along to ordinary investors?

Once specific constants are identified it becomes rather easy to follow Ralph Waldo Emerson's Roman rule. People who wish to become financially independent need only to copy or imitate the same constants employed by Buffett, Munger, and Franklin. What worked for them, in other words, will apply also to individuals today. That is the beauty of constants. They are not time or space specific. The constants of wealth creation work for all people in all ages and in all places where there is freedom to save and invest.

Warren Buffett's Paper Route

Warren Edward Buffett was born in August of 1930. Buffett often makes light of his birth. He fondly explains that his father was a stockbroker when the market crashed in October of 1929. Customers, after the great market crash, were reluctant to purchase securities, so his father started coming home early in the afternoons. The next thing you know, Warren Buffett appeared nine months later. Buffett notes that due to these personal circumstances, he has always held warm feelings about the stock market crash of 1929.[7]

Matters for the family at the time, however, were more serious. Buffett's dad lost his job at the bank when it closed just days before Warren's first birthday. Complicating matters further, his father's savings were exhausted. The country was rapidly plunging into the Great Depression of the 1930s.

Buffett's father responded to the crisis by opening his own brokerage firm, Buffett, Sklenicka & Co. His father was an independent thinker. He was also bold in his convictions. He was not afraid to establish a stock brokerage firm when pessimism on the markets was at its height. By the end of the 1930s decade, the Buffett family's fortunes had improved immensely. Buffett's father was elected to the U.S. House of Representatives on his first try in 1942. The Buffetts left Omaha, Nebraska, and moved to the outskirts of Washington, D.C.

The young Warren Buffett started early to capitalize on his independent thinking and tireless industry. He bought his first stock when just 11 years old by investing $114 in a single company. The investment went south, hitting $81, before recovering to $120. Buffett jumped at the chance to make a profit. He sold at $120, netting a $5 gain after commissions. Buffett then shifted wealth strategies. He moved away from owning common stocks and started applying his skills to where the real money was being made. He got a paper route. The young Buffett filed his first federal tax return at age 13, for his wages as a paperboy. The government was paid $7 income tax after a $35 deduction for a bicycle.

Roger Lowenstein, in his truly outstanding book, *Buffett: The Making of an American Capitalist,* meticulously details the extent of Buffett's commitment to industry during his teenage years. Two years after starting his paper route, Buffett transferred $1,200 from his earnings and bought 40 acres of Nebraska farmland. He rented the land to a tenant farmer for an extra source of income. Meanwhile, Buffett had increased the customer base of his paper route by expanding to five routes. Next he added a third business to his growing enterprise. He got into the pinball business. A friend had a knack for repairing used machines. Buffett supplied the capital and together they put the refurbished machines in barbershops. The pinball machines netted Buffett $50 a week, in addition to his paper route and farm income. Later on, Buffett added yet another business to the empire, selling secondhand golf balls. By the end of 1950, Buffett had saved $9,800 from his paper route, pinball machines, golf balls, and farmland investment.[8]

Warren Buffett graduated from high school at the age of 16. His father generously agreed to pay Warren's college tuition and expenses. "I was fortunate," said Buffett while speaking at a shareholder's meeting, "because my dad paid for my education. If he hadn't, I probably wouldn't have become educated if I'd had to pay for it myself."[9] The value of a college education was indeed more than just a rhetorical concern for Buffett. He was already generating meaningful cash flow from his four businesses. Further, he had read several books on business while in high school. Buffett, at age 16, questioned seriously, and somewhat legitimately, the future benefit of a college degree. He was just not sure there was that much more he could learn about business in college.

He resolved the dilemma by deferring to his father and enrolling in college. Buffett still, however, continued working and saving for much of his undergraduate career. While at the University of Nebraska at Lincoln, he worked one summer at JCPenney. Additionally, he kept the golf ball business alive while also managing 50 paperboys in six rural Nebraska counties while working for the *Lincoln Journal*.[10] Anxious to complete his undergraduate work as quickly as possible, Buffett rushed through his senior year by taking five courses in the fall, six courses in the spring, and three in the summer of 1950. He completed his degree in the summer of his 19th year.

Buffett promptly applied to Harvard's Graduate School of Business. Surprisingly, Harvard had no use for an enterprising kid who had built four businesses from the ground up and graduated from college years ahead of classmates. The rejection from Harvard, although disappointing, did little to deter Buffett. He bounced back and gained acceptance to Columbia. There he studied under the legendary professor, Benjamin Graham, author of *Security Analysis* and *The Intelligent Investor*. The experience at Columbia, specifically the interchange with Ben Graham, had a life-changing effect on Warren Buffett. Graham, wrote Buffett, "just lifted the scales from my eyes."[11]

Warren Buffett left Omaha in 1950 at the age of 20 with $9,800. He returned to Omaha for the last time in 1956. He was now 26 years old and independently wealthy. His $9,800 had grown to more than $140,000 within six years. Most of this same $9,800, of which more than half had come from his paper route earnings, would eventually grow to more than $40 billion ($40,000,000,000) within the next 55 years.

Because of his spectacular success as an investor, public statements made by Buffett are endlessly parsed by the media. Pundits search diligently for hidden revelations buried within his words. There are people who have actually paid more than $600,000 to have lunch with the Oracle of Omaha. (The money is generously donated to charity.) People want to know Buffett's thoughts on the dollar, the long bond, short rates, specific stocks, the Fed chairman, and the market in general. It must surely bemuse Buffett to know that crumbs from his table exceed the worth of golden loaves.

By observing the remarkable life of Warren Buffett, one learns that his fortunate lot in life arises from two sources: the circumstantial and the behavioral. The circumstantial factors are time, place, and person specific. The circumstantial is highly unlikely to ever be repeated by others. The behavioral factors, on the other hand, are predicated on certain beliefs and values and actions. It is possible for people to emulate or copy the behavioral factors.

Buffett's phenomenal investment performance since 1950 is circumstantial. That means it is improbable for any typical investor, regardless of skill or aptitude, to ever reproduce Buffett's investment performance over the past 56 years. One simply cannot teach what Buffett accomplished. It is much like reading a book on Albert Einstein and then trying to write an addendum to his theory of general relativity. The circumstantial is also not luck. The circumstantial is what a particular person can do in a particular situation with particular talents.

Trying to imitate Warren Buffett's investment results is a common and unfortunate mistake made by many new investors. They hear or read about Buffett and conclude that the key to becoming wealthy is to concentrate on achieving superior investment returns. They eventually discover the difficulty of trying to earn 24 percent a year on their investments. Meanwhile, they have lost time and often a lot of money. Sometimes they get discouraged and simply just throw in the towel. Attempting to duplicate Warren Buffett's investment performance is a very treacherous strategy for attaining financial independence. As stated, it is very difficult, if not impossible, to copy or imitate the circumstantial. Those obsessed with achieving superior investment results are nearly always following a perilous path.

On the other hand, the behavioral aspect of Warren Buffett's investing is determined by beliefs and values and actions that are possible for others to imitate. Buffett is a person of integrity. He is industrious, disciplined, and diligent. He does not scare easily; he is bold. Like his father, he is an independent thinker. He exercises patience; he will sometimes identify a particular stock and then wait years for the right price. He admits his mistakes and often seeks refuge in humor. He strives to stand above the crowd. The typical investor can emulate Buffett's core values, beliefs, and behavior. The encouraging truth is, Buffett's behavior of disciplined early saving and investing had already ensured him future wealth, or financial independence, even if he had never met Graham and adopted a systematic approach to investing. That $9,800 dollars he had saved as a young man and the disciplined saving lifestyle he led would have brought him to financial independence by itself, simply by the compounding of that money and his ongoing saving. While that acumen brought him unparalleled fortunes, he would still have experienced financial independence at retirement based on his early and disciplined saving.

Individuals, by their very natures, are seekers, and Warren Buffett was no exception. Various desires and interests drive most who journey through life. Sometimes these pursuits are spoken, and at other times they remain unspoken. Buffett, from an unusually early age, was never silent about his chief aim in life. He wanted to be rich; what's more, he believed he could be. When he was 12 years old, Buffett announced to Mary Falk, the wife of his father's business partner, that he was going to be a millionaire by age 30. "And if not," he added for dramatic measure, "I'm going to jump off the tallest building in Omaha."[12]

It becomes very difficult to assign one critical factor that has made all the difference in Warren Buffett's life. He is very intelligent, very focused, very driven, and extremely upright. When he made the decision to become rich, it was obvious to him and all who knew him that he would most likely get there. He, as I think most people readily acknowledge, is a person who possesses rare gifts. He was somehow born a professional.

And yet, as I reflect upon his great life, I keep coming back to that paper route of his. He bought his first stock at age 11 and even made some money doing so, but then he deemphasized investing. He changed strategies. He moved from working with his head and started working with his hands. Buffett worked feverishly throughout high school and most of college. Nearly everything earned was saved. Warren Buffett somehow figured out, at an incredibly young age, that all the investment acumen in the world is basically worthless unless one has seed money. In other words, until one has some real money, investing is little more than an academic exercise. To become rich, Buffett first needed money, so he withdrew from the stock market for a time and literally went to work. The second richest man in the country got his start by working not one, but by simultaneously working five paper routes while in high school.

Today there is so much of an emphasis on teaching workers who participate in 401(k) retirement plans how to invest. While most all investment knowledge is no doubt helpful, the effect of such education can be deemed only negligible as long as workers lack the seed money necessary to become wealthy. Buffett worked tirelessly to achieve $10,000 in seed money. Today's worker really needs more like $100,000. As we shall see in later chapters, until one first reaches $100,000 in retirement assets, the chances of retiring financially independent are not favorable. It requires a generous amount of seed money to get started on the road to wealth. This, I think, is the lesson that is so memorable when one thinks back to Warren Buffett's paper route.

Fortunately, the story of Warren Buffett's paper route is a lesson that can be copied or repeated by almost anyone. Seed money is produced by one's hands. Those desiring to achieve $100,000 in seed money as quickly as possible can take on an extra job, work overtime, or concentrate on moving up in their present career. There are all kinds of ways to earn and save extra money. Like peddling papers, it doesn't require a lot of sophistication to save, but personal focus, drive, and desire.

Warren Buffett was once asked by a teenage boy what advice he would give to a young person on how to be successful. Buffett answered, "It's better to hang out with people better than you. Pick out associates whose behavior is better than yours and you'll drift in that direction."[13]

Emulate that which can be copied, advises Buffett. Learn by standing. It works with the building of personal character and amazingly it works also with the building of personal wealth.

Charlie Munger's Yellow Pontiac

Once settled in Omaha in the late 1950s, Warren Buffett formed a partnership wherein he was investing money mostly for relatives. He was working with only $300,000, which was considered a modest sum for a money manager. One day the phone rang with a promising proposition on the other end. Edwin Davis, one the most prominent physicians in Omaha, wanted to meet Buffett.

Buffett quickly scheduled a meeting with Dr. Davis and his wife, Dorothy. Buffett came to the appointment wearing an oversized jacket. He talked fast and looked much younger than his actual age.[14] His appearance and bearing were unimpressive. Dr. Davis appeared completely disinterested in Buffett's sales pitch. He was hardly paying any attention. When Buffett finished, Dr. and Mrs. Davis huddled briefly and discussed the presentation. Mrs. Davis then informed Buffett they would like to invest $100,000. Buffett was flabbergasted. He said to Dr. Davis, "You weren't paying any attention. Why did you put money in?" Dr. Davis responded, "You remind me of Charlie Munger." Buffett remarked, "I don't know Charlie Munger but I like him already."[15]

Charlie Munger, like Buffett, grew up in Omaha. Munger is six years older than Buffett. Neither knew the other as teenagers or as young men, although Munger did work for a while in Buffett's grandfather's grocery store. Two years after securing Dr. Davis as a client, Buffett, at age 29, was introduced by the Davis family to Charlie Munger. They have remained close since their first dinner together in 1959. The chemistry between them was magic.

During his childhood, Charlie Munger's grandparents and parents prescribed to him the virtues of Daniel DeFoe and Benjamin Franklin. Munger recalls vivid memories of sitting with his grandmother and listening over and over to the story of *Robinson Crusoe*. The virtues of sacrifice, self-sufficiency, and independence would influence Munger for the remainder of his long life. He developed a passion for money as a means to independence.

Munger, after graduating from high school, enrolled at the University of Michigan and majored in mathematics. The outbreak of World War II, however, cut short his college career. Munger joined the army and trained to become a meteorologist at the California Institute of Technology in Pasadena. He soon was commissioned as an officer. Far removed from the action, as well as the comforts of civilization, Munger once harbored dreams when in the army of someday having "a lot of children, a house with lots of books, and enough money to have freedom."[16]

As a young man Munger was terribly impatient. He rushed headlong into marriage during the midst of war by marrying his sister's college roommate. His new bride was highly intelligent, but both were seemingly oblivious to the perilous mixture of war and passion and ill-thought-out dreams. Following the war, the still impatient Munger applied to Harvard Law School, even though he had not yet completed college. He was accepted and graduated magna cum laude in 1948.[17]

After law school, the Mungers returned to the West Coast with their children in tow. Munger passed the California bar in 1949 and joined a law firm. His dream of someday becoming wealthy with a house full of kids and books was slowly taking shape. By the early 1950s, Munger had three children and $1,500 in savings.[18]

Despite his intelligence, integrity, determination, and persistence, cracks were beginning to form and spread in Charlie Munger's life. First, Munger's marriage fell apart in 1953. Shortly thereafter, his home and most of his money were gone. Only one year later, his oldest child, and only son, was stricken with leukemia. Leukemia in the early 1950s was nearly always fatal. In those days, few families carried medical insurance. Munger just paid the bills. Teddy Munger died only a year after falling ill. "I can't imagine any experience in life worse than losing a child inch by inch," said Munger.[19] Like Benjamin Graham and Ben Franklin before him, Munger had lost his first-born son.

"You should never, when facing some unbelievable tragedy, let one tragedy increase to two or three through your failure of will,"[20] reflected Charlie Munger almost 50 years later. Obsession with heartache and disappointment, even when warranted, is nonetheless a sure path to defeat. Munger refused to dwell on the past. He forged ahead by continuing to focus on his same dreams and ambitions. He remarried, continued having children, persisted in spending less than his income, and buried himself in business interests. Munger was still in a hurry with destiny.

In her wonderful biography, *Damn Right! Behind the Scenes with Berkshire Hathaway Billionaire Charlie Munger,* Janet Lowe tells what has become one of my favorite stories about Charlie Munger. During his fight to get his life back on track, Munger was living in rented quarters. His car was a beat-up yellow Pontiac that had been cheaply repainted. He, according to his daughter, looked as though he did not have "two pennies to say hello to each other." Curious about her father's circumstances, Munger's daughter asked him, "Daddy, this car is just awful, a mess. Why do you drive it?" "To discourage gold diggers,"[21] he joked. Rather than worry his young daughter about the particulars of his personal circumstances, he, in typical Midwestern fashion, cracked a self-deprecating joke. Although he certainly could have taken out a loan and purchased a new car like so many others, he instead committed to the future, by under spending his income. He was driving an old car—not because he had to, but because it was his choice.

Munger sees the future value of money favorably because he understands investing. Investing, as explained by Warren Buffett, is "laying out money today to receive more money tomorrow."[22] "That's what investment is," says Munger. "You don't spend the money—even though there are a lot of lovely things you can buy with it. You may even *sacrifice* something—because you're trying to do better later."[23] Munger's wife of 50 years once remarked that Munger "was a young man in a hurry."[24] People who typically hurry through life do so because they anticipate something good at the other end. This observation by Munger's wife is one very important key to understanding his success at building personal wealth. Charlie Munger could concentrate effectively on the future.

There are many Americans today who find themselves where Munger once stood. Some have made mistakes. Others have perhaps suffered misfortune. Many were maybe just unprepared. There are, nonetheless, literally millions of workers who now face retirement with insufficient savings. They are either behind the curve or altogether off the track.

The moving story of Charlie Munger's early years makes evident to individual investors that the path to financial independence is seldom straight. There are numerous twists and turns and unanticipated setbacks. Long stretches of dry, parched road are not uncommon. It often is a fight. When Munger was 30 years old with his savings depleted, he knew exactly what he had to do. First, he had to start all over again. Second, he had to under spend his income so he would have money to invest.

This meant he would have to keep driving the secondhand Pontiac for a while longer.

The yellow Pontiac, from my perspective, symbolizes Charlie Munger's unfailing belief in the wealth-creation process. He truly believed he could become wealthy, perhaps even rich. Wealth creation, as mentioned earlier, is a self-controlled process. Financial independence, in other words, is often determined by the inner person. The irony of Charlie Munger's early professional years is that he actually had the means to maintain a pretense of looking wealthy. He was, after all, a Harvard-educated attorney with a secure job. But Charlie Munger did not want to simply appear wealthy; he wanted to be wealthy. Even though circumstances had moved his goal farther away from him, he pressed onward. He remained with his yellow Pontiac and kept driving to financial independence.

Speaking at an annual shareholders meeting at Wesco Financial in California, Munger reminded the audience that "a lot of success in life and business comes from knowing what you really want to avoid."[25] The possibility of facing an uncertain retirement future with insufficient savings is one such prospect facing millions of Americans. There is no magic to becoming wealthy over time. The road to wealth, as demonstrated by Warren Buffett and Charlie Munger, can be fairly predictable. Avoiding the future prospect of insufficient funds available at retirement is one clear incentive for getting started now on the road to wealth.

Benjamin Franklin's Diet

Benjamin Franklin is one of the most original, intriguing, and significant figures in American history. During his life span, he was an inventor, politician, businessman, author, diplomat, and scientist. He invented the lightning rod, bifocal eyeglasses, the Franklin stove, and glass harmonica, for which even Mozart and Beethoven composed music.[26] He signed the Declaration of Independence, and the U.S. Constitution, served as the president of Pennsylvania, and was America's first postmaster general. An entrepreneur, Franklin built one of the most prosperous printing companies in the colonies and became a best-selling author with his *Poor Richard's Almanac.* Prior to the Declaration of Independence, he represented several of the colonies as the official agent to Parliament. Following the Declaration of Independence, he was an ambassador to

France, where he successfully secured funding for the Continental army. His work with electricity won him coveted acclaim from leading scientists and philosophers throughout the world, including Scotsman David Hume, Irishman Edmund Burke, German Immanuel Kant, Italian Giambattista Beccarin, and Frenchman Voltaire.[27] "I, for one, am better because I learned from Franklin's life," asserts Charlie Munger.[28]

Franklin's life story began in humble origin. His early years were difficult, complex, and, in many respects, troubling. His father immigrated to Boston from England, where he established a profitable candle shop. Franklin had 13 surviving brothers and sisters; he was the youngest son. His formal schooling ceased when Franklin was only 10. He started working, with only two years of childhood education, for his father. Franklin found the work dreadful. Unlike the appealing and sweetly scented candle and soap shops of today, chandlers in the 18th century were subject to almost unbearable working conditions. The smell of boiled animal fats permeated the shop. It was an awful way to earn a living.

Franklin's older brother, James, soon found a solution. James agreed, along with his father's consent, to hire Benjamin as an apprentice. Franklin, at age 12, signed an indentured agreement that legally bound him to his brother, who was a printer, for an unusually long nine years. Franklin agreed to room and board and training, with no wages paid until the ninth and final year of the contract. The young Franklin would not receive a cent for his labors until the age of 21.

Franklin, like Buffett and Munger, did not roll down a gentle slope to financial independence. At the outset, prosperity appeared impossible. Practically an indentured servant with no income, he was simply not in a position to break out financially. Conventional wisdom would have one believe it was not his lot in life to start quickly.

The clever Franklin, however, thought otherwise. He read a book on the advantages of vegetarianism. He reasoned the absence of beef and pork from his diet would reduce the overall cost of his board by half. James agreed to the proposition, and since he now didn't have to pay for Franklin's meat, paid that money to Franklin instead. Franklin pocketed the savings. He had monetized his diet and demonstrated as a teenager that one can effectively under spend income without even receiving wages.

Franklin took the money earned from his diet and invested in books. He read voraciously. It made little sense for him to bother joining the others during mealtime, so he remained in the shop and read. His knowledge base expanded and his writing skills improved immeasurably. He eventually equaled, and then began challenging, his older brother intellectually. Not only was the young Franklin getting ahead financially, his cognitive skills were also rapidly expanding. Remarkably, Franklin's diet was not only producing seed money for future wealth, but seeds to his genius were beginning to sprout as well.

It was just a matter of time before sibling rivalries erupted in the print shop. The two brothers first began sparring verbally, before the fighting turned physical. James, who was nine years older than Benjamin, was easily able to handle the younger Franklin. The beatings, by some accounts, were brutal. The working conditions deteriorated. Life in the print shop was intolerable for Benjamin.

Franklin, fed up with the mistreatment, decided to flee. His situation was more precarious than the typical teenager running away from home because Franklin still had several years remaining on his contract. He would therefore be a fugitive and, if apprehended, subject to punishment. The determined Franklin nonetheless hatched a plot. He decided to leave Boston by ship. To secure passage as a minor, he fabricated a mischievous tale. He then dispatched an equally impish friend to meet with the ship's captain on Franklin's behalf. The friend explained to the captain that Franklin "had got a naughty girl with child"[29] and her family was pressuring him to get married. The worldly captain bought into the hoax. The captain took the money Franklin had saved and looked the other way when he boarded.

Weeks later the 17-year-old Franklin arrived in Philadelphia. He knew absolutely no one. He had no place to stay and what remained of his savings was meager. There were two printers in town. He called on both of them. The first was a good businessman, but, unbelievably enough, illiterate. The second possessed sufficient education, but was a horrible businessman. The printer lacking business acumen offered Franklin work.

Franklin's proficiency, within the year, caught the attention of William Keith, governor of Pennsylvania. Governor Keith expressed dismay over the quality and aptitude of those printers currently in Philadelphia. He encouraged Franklin to embark on his own and establish a third shop to compete with the other two. The precocious Franklin overwhelmingly concurred with Governor Keith's assessment. Franklin, however, was a teenage fugitive without money. When Franklin failed to secure funding from his family in Boston, Governor Keith suggested that Franklin travel to London, where the governor would arrange financing with his overseas contacts.

The teenage Franklin was utterly flattered. He set forth immediately for London. Once in London, Franklin unfortunately discovered that Governor Keith was without financial contacts. William Keith was just simply a bombastic talker, and Franklin, in a vain attempt to get rich quick, fell for Keith's hyperbole. Franklin foolishly succumbed to the age-old trap of believing what he wanted to hear.

Franklin returned to America humiliated. He was disappointed in both himself and the character of Governor William Keith. Impoverished, with little evidence that he would ever succeed in life, Franklin refused to acknowledge personal defeat. He took out a piece of paper and a pen on the voyage home and pledged devotion to these words:

> To apply myself industriously to whatever business I take in hand, and not divert my mind from my business by any foolish project of growing suddenly rich; for industry and patience are the surest means of plenty.[30]

Great people often make horrible mistakes. Franklin was no exception to this rule. Riding back on that ship to America, it is unlikely any of the other passengers realized the urchin on board would someday become the most widely adored man in America, if not the world. Big mistakes build great people whenever they are able to climb up from the canvas and keep fighting. Franklin became wealthy not because he was always able to sidestep misfortune, but because failure made him smarter. He learned by standing.

The story of Franklin's teenage years bears two very important lessons for our modern times. Both of these lessons are straightforward and easily understood. Today, for example, there are many who earn wages and yet claim there is not money enough left over to save. The young Franklin had no wages and was likewise also unable to save. And then one day, despite the fact that he still earned no wages, Franklin figured out a way to save. Franklin solved this problem not by some great stroke of brilliance or by "thinking outside the box." Instead, Franklin solved the problem of insufficient savings through a willingness to change. In this case, he changed his diet. We learn from the teenage Franklin that savings are determined sometimes not so much by external factors such as wages, occupations, or circumstances, but rather by internal considerations surrounding a willingness to change. Change, in other words, is one catalyst for saving.

Getting lured overseas by Governor Keith marked the second critical lesson in Franklin's young life. When confronted with his first major setback, Franklin did not recoil, but rather demonstrated tenacity. Forgoing blame, Franklin assumed full responsibility for his actions. Ambitious and impatient to establish his mark upon society, he had fallen subject to insolence. Franklin acknowledged his failure, accepted the consequences, made a plan for the future, and, incredibly enough, remained committed to those precepts for the rest of his life.

Twenty-three years after being duped by Governor Keith, Franklin attained financial independence and retired from the printing business. Franklin followed a plan that was straightforward and succinct. Financially independent at the age of 42, after building ownership in a business, Franklin was now free to pursue his scientific interests and political ambitions. It is quite possible that had Benjamin Franklin been unwilling to change his diet and unable to recover so completely from his first major disappointment at age 19, his genius may well have been hidden from the world and history.

Start Now, Save Sufficient Sums, Invest Wisely

There are many similarities to be found among Warren Buffett, Charlie Munger, and Benjamin Franklin. All became financially independent while rather young. Each achieved greatness and was known and revered nationally. All were courageous, self-reliant, introspective, fiercely independent, and amused as well as sustained by humor. They shunned mediocrity. All were tempered by disappointment. None placed limits on his potential. Buffett, Munger, and Franklin, when measured against any standard of human endeavor, are all singularly extraordinary.

Among the numerous and varied similarities of Buffett, Munger, and Franklin, however, are at least three constants every investor can emulate. The difficult question facing millions of workers today is, How does one become wealthy? The answer is found in these three constants: Start now, save sufficient sums, and invest wisely. Those with the determination to do these things are likely to have a lock on becoming wealthy whatever their position in the workplace. Conventional wisdom would, of course, suggest otherwise. Conventional wisdom maintains that people tend to become wealthy whenever they secure high-paying jobs, achieve spectacular investment returns, and receive a fair share of lucky breaks. There obviously is some measure of truth in this as high wages, superior investment returns, and good luck can all contribute to personal wealth creation. But the overwhelming truth is that wealth creation does not depend on lucky breaks, but is rather the natural and dependable result of starting now, saving sufficient sums, and investing wisely.

Charlie Munger is fond of quoting the great algebraist Carl Jacobi, who notes that whenever someone is trying to solve a difficult problem, one should "invert, always invert."[31] Wisely applied to the wealth creation issue, it looks like this: What doesn't work when one is trying to become wealthy? People who fail to become wealthy start late, save too little, and make poor investment decisions. Those who procrastinate, overspend, and make lousy investment choices typically do not become wealthy over a working lifetime. Surprisingly, the average American worker has nearly every advantage as the executive in the corner suite when it comes, then, to the business of wealth creation. Those who start now, save sufficient sums, and invest wisely are likely to become wealthy over time, regardless of their starting point. Workers who perform these three tasks stand equal to the intelligent-sounding and often-intimidating Wall Street strategists who appear on television and in print all the time. The mystery of wealth creation is not that complicated. Start now. Save sufficient sums. Invest wisely.

CHAPTER 3

The Constants

What maintains one vice would bring up two children.
Benjamin Franklin

Those Who Believe Start Now

When people truly believe they can become wealthy, they start the wealth-creation process by saving aggressively. Because 401(k) plans offer workers a near-perfect platform to build wealth over time, it always seemed to me that every worker eligible to participate in a 401(k) plan would want to do so at the first opportunity. It just made sense. That, however, is rarely the case. I have personally observed countless 401(k) enrollment meetings over the years. I know the numbers well. One out of four employees doesn't sign up. Many others just barely get their toes wet. The excuses offered for not enrolling are endless. I remember one man even standing up in front of his fellow workers and exclaiming he could not enroll because he was supporting eight ex-wives. Many who do not enroll pledge that they will get on board at the next meeting. They are just not ready to start now. Starting now, oddly enough, is difficult for people.

Only a minority of people saves truly significant sums. Most who do save are not saving nearly enough to become financially independent. Watching those in the audience closely has taught me that most of them speak a very clear message through their eyes and facial expressions. Although hardly anyone brings down the house with laughter like the fellow claiming to have eight ex-wives, the essential message is often the same. Many are just not ready to commit.

The real world where people work and live their lives is comprised of concrete numbers that provide a certain sense of predictability. For instance, people have some idea what to expect when the light bill arrives. Most individuals are generally inclined to make commitments when there is some degree of certainty, which is one reason bank-insured certificates of deposit (CDs) are such popular investments. This particular type of investment fits the real-world picture very well. A person hands over money for a specific period of time with a defined rate of return and a guarantee that all the money plus earnings will be returned. This is the type of predictability that facilitates commitment.

Company 401(k) plans offer workers tremendous benefits. These plans are ideal vehicles for the creation of personal wealth. Money is subtracted from an employee's paycheck and then deposited into that same employee's personal savings account each pay period. Employee money deposited into the 401(k) account is not initially taxed by the government, which creates a sort of government-subsidized savings program. The earnings grow tax deferred until participants withdraw the money at retirement. Sometimes employers will even match the employee savings with additional corporate money. Mutual funds or index funds are the usual investments of choice in these savings programs. Thus, 401(k) plans offer participants a platform wherein it is possible for workers to become self-made millionaires.

It is important for workers as they prepare to enroll in a 401(k) plan to clearly understand the real-world numbers involved. First, the purpose of these programs is to make individual, everyday workers wealthy by retirement age. These are not Christmas club savings accounts. These programs are also not to be understood as government-subsidized, personal, discretionary savings accounts wherein one can tap into his or her very own pool of tax-advantaged assets to buy a boat or motorcycle or vacation home. These programs are vehicles for the creation of financial independence. These accounts are designed for the specific purpose of someday replacing your job. The money in these accounts needs to be sufficient enough to maintain your standard of living until the day you and your spouse die, without ever having to worry about running out of money. When viewed from the perspective of the real world, these are very serious programs for the placement of very serious money that requires a very serious commitment.

The individual retirement goal in a 401(k) program is really nothing more than the value of a person's job. Your job is worth a lot of money, more than many people realize. For example, if you are earning $35,000, it takes about $700,000, or 20 times your income, to replace your job in today's dollars. When planning for retirement, the value is much higher because of the effect of inflation. These are real-world numbers that demand serious consideration. Those who do not plan and prepare to replace the monetary value of their jobs may have no other alternative but to keep on working in retirement.

When enrolling in 401(k) plans, people need to know these real-world numbers. They need to know, for example, how to determine a financial goal for retirement. They need to know how to measure savings progress. And, most importantly, they need to know how much money they must start saving now. It is rather obvious that those who do not understand the purpose of these savings programs or the amount of money one must put away each pay period to retire financially independent will likely finish well short of the goal.

Later chapters will outline clearly the numbers investors must know to retire wealthy. It seems only reasonable that before workers can be expected to commit themselves to starting now, these same people must understand the financial requirements of participating in 401(k) plans. Whenever the message of starting now and saving sufficient sums is either vague or evasive in the employee enrollment meetings, the ultimate cost to participants is severe. It is a mistake to believe workers will make long-term commitments when real-world numbers are absent.

A theme that will resonate throughout this book is the clarity of numbers. Benjamin Franklin understood well, while still a teenager, the monetary value of a print shop. I would guess Charlie Munger could have quantified what it would take for him to become financially independent. And Warren Buffett knew what would have to happen for him to become a millionaire at a very young age. When you finish this book, you will also know how much money you need to have put away for retirement. You will know what you must start saving now.

There is hardly a day that passes now whereby one does not read about a traditional defined benefit pension plan being terminated. These traditional pension plans are usually replaced with 401(k) plans. The obligation to save is being shifted from the employer to the employee. Knowing how to set a goal and determine the amount one must save each pay period is perhaps now more than ever commonly recognized as a vital aspect to the success of these individual savings programs.

Less obvious, but no less real, is the independence that also is shifting to individual workers. All the money workers put into their 401(k) accounts belongs unconditionally to them. It is placed in a special trust and can *never* be taken away. Even if a worker gets sued or goes bankrupt, 401(k) money is still there for that worker's retirement. Workers who participate in 401(k) plans own the assets. And, importantly, workers can take these personal retirement assets with them should they ever change jobs. Workers who save for retirement in their 401(k) plans control the process of individual wealth creation.

People who believe they will become wealthy start saving now. They place complete trust in the process of wealth creation and in themselves. Curiously, it does not require discipline to start, but those who complete the process of under spending and creating wealth eventually become well disciplined. It is the same with patience. Patience is not a prerequisite for starting, but invariably, those who finish wealthy are patient investors. Starting now, however, does demand a tremendous amount of conviction. An individual who starts now stands firm in the belief that one can become wealthy. It is a serious venture. It is a sound decision that unites the ordinary investor with Buffett, Munger, and Franklin through the very same spirit of optimism and faith in ownership that forever changed their lives.

People Who Become Wealthy
Save Sufficient Sums

Earning modest to low wages is one of the most common and compelling reasons offered for not starting and not saving. Many with moderate to low incomes do not even consider putting money away for retirement because of the belief that saving confers a horrible hardship on the individual. For example, whenever one ventures into a grocery store, a gallon of milk, tube of toothpaste, pound of butter, or a box of cereal is not priced on a variable scale that considers one's annual income. The sales clerk who earns minimum wage pays the same price for a gallon of milk as does the wealthiest person in America. (Interestingly, the wealthiest person in America cannot buy a better gallon of milk or tube of toothpaste than the poorest American.) Because, however, goods and services necessary for survival are not priced relative to income, lower wage earners often subscribe to a common stereotype that saving is futile. Saving, to them, makes no difference: Unless one is highly paid, it is unlikely to ever become independently wealthy.

A recent statistic published in *BusinessWeek* reported that 28 percent of Americans say that once they have paid their essential living expenses, they have "no spare cash."[1] Although the survey did not define what constitutes "essential" living expenses, the point is clear. There are a great number of Americans who find it difficult, perhaps even impossible, to save because they are completely tapped out by the basic costs of living. These Americans could not save, even if they wanted to, because of the perception that there is not money enough to do so.

It is strangely curious that had this same survey been conducted 285 years ago, Benjamin Franklin, an indentured servant with no income, would not have been counted among those unable to save. Franklin, as noted earlier, figured out a way to save even though he was not being paid a cent for his labors. There is no question that it is difficult for lower-paid workers to start now and save. Low wages, however, must not be accepted as a valid excuse for not saving. Fortunately, low-wage earners have been shown to be just as likely as high-wage earners to become wealthy over time, whenever they start early, under spend, and invest. Low wages, in other words, do not prohibit individuals from becoming wealthy. It is rather the failure to start early, save, and invest that precludes the accumulation of personal wealth. Individuals, regardless of their profession or annual income, can—with a high degree of predictability—become wealthy over a working lifetime whenever these three very repeatable tasks are successfully implemented and executed.

Scholarly studies are beginning to emerge that support the claim that individual wealth accumulated over a working lifetime is indeed predicated upon the completion of repeatable actions or tasks. Steven F. Venti and David A. Wise, in an excellent research piece entitled "Choice, Chance, and Wealth Dispersion at Retirement," make the cogent case that individual choice is the primary factor separating those with money at retirement from those who have little or none. The research by Venti and Wise refutes many of the conventional stereotypes surrounding poverty and wealth. It is the individual choice to get started and save, according to these researchers, that determines whether people are able to accumulate meaningful financial assets.

It is not surprising that most who either lack significant financial assets or have little understanding of wealth, have subscribed to conventional thinking. For example, many are inclined to believe the stereotype that those who have higher-paying jobs find it much easier to save and accumulate wealth than those who have lower-paying jobs. Venti and Wise's research, however, refutes this common claim. They instead discovered that "in the United States it is not only households with low incomes that save little. A significant proportion of high-income households also save very little."[2]

Statistical analysis conducted by Venti and Wise supported the finding that sometimes the best savers from low-income households had more money put away at retirement than the worst savers from high-income groups in America. Those who earn high wages must still make the conscious choice to save; otherwise, they may very well face retirement with insufficient financial resources. Venti and Wise strongly support the belief that those with low wages can acquire significant financial assets over a working lifetime, if the decision is made early on to first initiate and then continue saving. Insufficient income at retirement does not necessarily result from poor wages. The absence of wealth at retirement is often the result of not starting to save early enough in life.

The implications of Venti and Wise's research are truly astonishing. Their findings not only challenge, but actually reverse decades of erroneous assumptions surrounding financial independence. First, according to Venti and Wise, low-wage earners can accumulate meaningful sums of money over time. Their findings conclusively support the notion that one does not have to start with money to become financially secure in America. Wealth is primarily determined by the choice to save,[3] not the chance of someday earning high wages. Second, and perhaps more significantly, low-income wage earners who save throughout their lifetimes will have accumulated greater wealth at retirement age than higher-wage earners who did not save. In other words, a person's income is not the final word on whether a person will ever accrue meaningful financial assets in life.

Benjamin Franklin is a valuable role model for millions of Americans who wish to someday become wealthy. He, as we learned earlier, financed his saving by becoming a vegetarian. The benefits, curiously, were numerous. First, he now had money to invest. Second, he gained a healthier lifestyle. Third, because it made little sense to join the others at mealtime, he remained behind in the shop and read. Time away from the presses and the boarding table was applied to education. Finally, and most significantly, under spending further strengthened and disciplined Franklin's will to succeed in life. His decision to under spend created an unforeseen chain reaction of positive results. Ben Franklin's life improved immeasurably as a consequence of his determination to start early and save.

There are many who face the prospect of under spending their incomes with much trepidation. They fear that under spending will take something valuable away. It seemingly runs counter to human nature to voluntarily surrender or relinquish rights, privileges, and possessions. We learn from Franklin, however, that under spending can spark creativity. Saving often focuses the mind so that certain benefits spill over into other areas of one's life. Not to belabor the point, but people must be careful to not fall into the shortsighted trap of thinking that saving and under spending inflict hardship because of the perception that something is being given up. Like Franklin, it is very possible to experience a chain reaction of unanticipated positive results when saving.

In his book, *The Way to Wealth*, Benjamin Franklin poignantly underscores the many advantages of under spending one's income. Franklin argues rather convincingly that much of what people count as necessities could hardly pass as even conveniences. People, in other words, have a natural propensity to unwittingly waste money and then confuse their self-imposed negligence with hardship. "What maintains one vice," observes Franklin, "would bring up two children."[4]

Life in the colonies during the 1700s was difficult. There was very little money. Most families bartered those goods essential for survival. Further, basic necessities were sparse; luxuries were exceedingly uncommon. There were no safety nets other than charity or the kindness of strangers. The inability to repay debts could land a person in serious trouble. Financial carelessness could ruin a family. Eighteenth-century America was unusually cold and cruel by today's standards.

Remarkably, Benjamin Franklin was able to see through the genuine hardship and undeniable disadvantages of colonial times and figure out how ordinary families could actually attain financial independence. Franklin's understanding of personal wealth creation was one of the period's most revolutionary discoveries. Wealth, implied Franklin, was not the exclusive province of kings and queens and princes and those privileged by birth into aristocracy. Wealth was also well within the reach of common, ordinary people. Conventional wisdom, nonetheless, weighed heavily against Franklin's precepts. Most thought the prospects of ordinary people learning to become wealthy to be unequivocally absurd. Born into anonymity, penniless, and a complete stranger to everyone in Philadelphia at the age of 17, Franklin was financially independent by the age of 42. It was not because of luck or good fortune, either. Franklin's "way to wealth" was very repeatable. Anyone, and this is the crucial key, *anyone* can copy or emulate the necessary tasks of personal wealth creation. Wealth, in this regard, is extremely democratic.

Those Who Become Wealthy Invest Wisely

There are those who believe that one must outperform the stock market in order to become financially independent. This is a myth. Concentrating on achieving above-average investment returns, ironically enough, is very dangerous business. It has ruined countless investors. It is exceedingly difficult to outperform the averages when investing in the stock market. In his excellent book, *Winning the Loser's Game,* Charles Ellis notes, "The historical record is that in the 25 years ending with 1997, on a cumulative basis, over three-fourths of professionally managed funds under performed the S&P 500 Market Stock Average."[5] Amateur investors who set out to beat the market are asking for trouble. "For most of us," writes Jeremy Siegel, author of *Stocks for the Long Run,* "trying to beat the market leads to disastrous results."[6] That is not to say someone cannot become the next Warren Buffett or Charlie Munger, but the odds of doing so are spectacularly long. As mentioned earlier, Buffett's investment performance since 1950 is hardly repeatable. There are many, many wonderful attributes of Warren Buffett that can and should be emulated when becoming wealthy, but trying to copy his investment performance is not one of them. As peculiar or counterintuitive as it sounds, the goal when investing in the stock market, especially for amateur investors, is to shoot for average or normal returns. Those who try to perform better than the averages, often take on greater than average risks.

Then, when things do not work out, they get into trouble and suffer needless losses. Average or normal investment performance over the long term is generally very good news for the ordinary investor.

Years ago I received an invitation to join the managment team at a Wall Street investment firm in New York City. One day, soon after arriving in town and while getting acclimated to life in the city and corporate headquarters, I noticed an older veteran of the street selling every single share of stock he owned. Curious as to why this executive was liquidating his portfolio, I inquired further. He responded that he had been buying and selling individual stocks in his personal account for more than 20 years, but had failed to make any real money investing on his own. He had finally come to the conclusion that the only way he was ever going to make money was to sell everything he now owned, cease trading stocks, and put all of his assets into a mutual fund. Completely new to the ways of Wall Street, I couldn't have been more surprised. It had always been my impression that access to the ways of Wall Street was a sure advantage over the everyday investor.

"One of the hardest things to imagine is that you are not smarter than average," said Daniel Kahneman, who was awarded the 2002 Nobel Prize for his work in economic science.[7] The executive who was selling everything to buy shares of a mutual fund taught me a very valuable lesson. He in effect was saying that individuals cannot outsmart the stock market. Years of experiencing unsatisfactory investment returns had finally led him to conclude that it was good to be an average investor.

Our culture places a very low premium on average. No one wants to be average. Average, however, is sometimes greatly misunderstood. There are at least two dimensions to being average. One is the commonly understood dimension of mediocrity. When something is very highly valued by someone, mediocre or average is completely unacceptable. For example, when a person is interviewing for a very important position, that individual obviously does not want to leave an impression of being just average. A quarterback playing in a championship bowl on national television does not want to have an average game. A gourmet cook never wants to prepare an average meal for guests. Average is generally perceived negatively. There are times, however, when even overachievers want to be average. Average is typically a good thing when visiting the doctor. When the physician checks a patient's blood sugar, average is great. It is the same with blood pressure. Average at the doctor's office is not just good news, it's fabulous news. Few things are more welcome than hearing the words *normal* or *average* from a physician.

The primary objective of investing is not to outperform the stock market, but rather to achieve important financial goals in life.[8] The chief aim of starting now and saving and investing is to become financially independent by retirement age. The process typically takes the better part of a working lifetime. Achieving average or normal investment returns, or keeping pace with broad stock market indexes over such a long time period, is more than sufficient for the attainment of personal wealth. In other words, the thing that will kill you in the market is not average or normal returns, but below-average or inferior performance. I have never met a person who failed to retire because his or her performance in the stock market achieved normal returns over time. I have met people, however, who were just miserable because their experiences in the market were below par.

Stocks represent ownership in a company. A stock shareholder actually owns a part of the company. The stock shareholder therefore has rights to the profits of the company. Charlie Munger has often said that to become wealthy one must build ownership in a business. Purchasing shares of stock is one way for ordinary investors to build legitimate ownership in a company.

Sometimes ordinary investors are not sure which specific companies to own. This is a rather common concern among individuals. To help solve this problem, investment companies put together mutual funds. Mutual funds are professionally managed accounts that invest in a number of stocks or companies. Mutual funds will typically own stock in anywhere from 50 to 100 different companies. The risk of owning just a single stock is reduced through diversification, which means that whenever one purchases a mutual fund, the investor actually owns shares in 50 to 100 different companies. When Warren Buffett talks about index funds, he is referring to a type of mutual fund that invests in a particular basket of stocks comprising a certain stock index, such as the Standard & Poor's (S&P) 500 (500 of the largest companies in the United States) or the Russell 2000 (2,000 smaller, U.S. publicly held companies). Mutual funds or index funds are another way to build legitimate ownership in a business.

Warren Buffett has said on more than one occasion that people who are unsure of what they are doing ought to just buy an index fund. "Investors need to avoid the negatives of buying fads, crummy companies, and timing the market," says Buffett. "Buying an index fund over a long period of time makes the most sense."[9] Buffett is no doubt familiar with the math on index funds. Had Buffett purchased an index fund comprised of large capitalization stocks with his $9,800 in 1950, he incredibly enough would still have eventually become a multi-millionaire.

Investors can realize a normal or average investment return by purchasing shares in either an index fund or reputable mutual fund with a long investment record demonstrating normal returns. One does not have to shoot the lights out to become wealthy. Average gets the job done just fine. And average, strangely enough, is all it takes for ordinary investors to keep pace with most professionals when it comes to investing in the stock market.

Professional Investment Partners

There is a common characteristic that seems to always be present among professionals: They seldom travel alone. Whenever physicians experience personal medical problems, they are quick to get on the phone and consult close friends within the profession. It is the same with lawyers. One seldom sees an attorney representing him- or herself in court. They instead seek valued counsel from colleagues. Few ever achieve excellence solely on their own merit. Few athletes, for example, become great without tremendous coaches. Lifetime goals are most easily attained when working in concert with others.

The goal of personal wealth creation is very doable for most workers who start now, save sufficient sums, and invest wisely. The path, however, is not straight. There are long stretches when the way is difficult and uncertain. It is an emotional journey. Those who travel this road face times of sheer panic, periods of euphoria, and sometimes years of boredom. It is not a road, for the solitary traveler.

Several years ago, following the tech bubble of 2000, there was a televised Senate hearing in Washington, D.C. A company had gone bankrupt. Those employees who had put all their 401(k) retirement savings into this particular company stock got wiped out. The stock fell to zero, and thousands of participant account balances followed the equity all the way into oblivion. The Senators paraded a steady stream of devastated employees before the committee to testify on national television. It was a very sad day. Gone were lifetime after lifetime of retirement dreams.

The testimonies were very emotional. Many of the employees were so sad they could hardly speak. Quite a few were choking and trying to hold back tears. It was amazing how many of these ordinary workers had lost hundreds of thousands of dollars. The losses were just incredible. The Senators were emotional as well. Some were angry. A few were even noticeably outraged. Although they could not replace the millions of lost dollars and thousands of retirement dreams, this particular Senate committee vowed to get to the bottom of the matter and pass some more laws to protect 401(k) participants.

Lost in the hysteria was the fact that based upon the evidence presented at this particular Senate hearing, the company 401(k) plan that supposedly destroyed the retirement wealth of so many employees, was actually a fairly decent retirement plan. Each of the employees who were wiped out had the choice of also investing in well-diversified mutual funds. Some of these funds were completely unaffected by the company stock meltdown. A very important point, lost in the emotion of the testimony, was that there was no need for such awful financial carnage. The problem was not completely with the company. The fault was also not totally with the company-sponsored 401(k) plan. The problem, as Shakespeare put it, often "lies . . . in ourselves."[10]

The road to wealth is sometimes an anxious journey. The stock of this particular company, before the bottom fell out, was going through the roof. The 401(k) participants had the option of buying company stock within the retirement plan. Euphoria and innuendo just simply swept the employees away. Those who got wiped out sold every cent of their mutual funds and jumped on the company stock bandwagon. They were getting rich quickly. It apparently never occurred to those who had placed their entire retirement nest egg in a single, highflying stock that the world just doesn't work this way. Few, if any, had put together an exit strategy. The party, they erroneously thought, would simply go on forever. They unfortunately were very wrong.

One should never underestimate the power of emotion when traveling the road to wealth. Fear and greed, terror and euphoria, volatility and long stretches of boredom can destroy fortunes. There is no law the U.S. Senate is capable of ever passing that can fully protect investors from their folly and exposure to emotion. Emotion eventually visits all investors. No one is immune. Astute investors, however, seldom travel alone. It, in a sense, is the fourth constant. Individual investors who travel the road of wealth creation are wise and usually well served when they partner with a financial professional.

Listening to the Senate testimony of those who had lost everything, one was left with the clear impression that these employees were all alone in their travels on the road to wealth. There was no one on the outside, far removed from the euphoria and misleading assurances of management, to impart a differing perspective. Amazingly, the right answer was right in front of everyone, and yet few were able to see the value of long-term investing through well-diversified mutual funds that were available to each participant. Instead, the great majority seemed to have been converted at the water cooler, where stories of the real money getting made got circulated. It is doubtful, in fact extremely doubtful, that any financial professional with an appreciation for diversification and the preservation of capital would ever encourage 401(k) participants to put every last cent of their retirement savings in a single, high-flying stock.

The purpose of a 401(k) plan is to make every single participant who saves and invests wealthy by retirement age. It is serious business. Participants should not just have access to financial professionals, but meaningful and personal partnerships with these persons. Each journey requires one to travel an individual path with unique challenges and dreams. The assembly line works fine when manufacturing cupcakes, but not personal financial freedom. Workers should never be in doubt as to where they are going, how they are getting there, and with whom they are sharing responsibility for their future livelihood.

PART TWO

Start Now and
Save Sufficient Sums

CHAPTER 4

The First
Million Dollars

There's really nothing to it.
Richard Branson

Form and Structure

It was once said that there have been no philosophers since Plato. Plato lived nearly 2,500 years ago in ancient Greece. He observed the world and the human condition, and then devised a structure that outlined humanity's role in the universe. Plato created a form or pattern that served as a guideline for understanding human behavior. He addressed the crucial questions of human existence. It has been said that there have been no philosophers since Plato because no one has done more to explain humanity's role in the unfolding history of Western civilization.

Plato thought it made a lot of sense to first figure out the form and structure of a particular problem before jumping headlong into the process of solving it. For instance, before someone starts saving hard-earned money from each paycheck and putting this money into the stock market or mutual funds, it benefits that investor to first discern how wealth is created. Are there certain principles of wealth creation that always seem to hold true? Are there certain behaviors that predestine trouble? Plato, when contemplating any of the deep mysteries of the universe, always tried to paint a picture or create a mental image of the problem or mystery in need of understanding. This is what is meant by form and structure. It is nothing more than a mental image or picture.

Once Plato could figure out a mental image or a picture to a problem or one of life's mysteries, he could then find the proper solution or answer.

Today, there are 45 million workers who participate in 401(k) retirement programs. These workers have several trillion dollars invested in these plans. Billions of new dollars pour into these accounts annually. And yet, very few workers can answer the most basic questions of personal retirement planning. For example, take the following question: How much money should someone my age, with my income, have put away already for retirement? This is hardly a trick question. It is a basic question and requires only an elementary understanding of wealth creation to answer correctly. There are, however, only a small fraction of 401(k) participants who can correctly answer this practical question, which is fundamental to the whole process of financial independence. It is a classic example of the cart getting out in front of the horse. Workers have been asked to jump headlong into a process wherein there often is very little understanding or proficiency on the part of participants. Based on Plato's methodology, it would indeed make sense to first have a mental image or picture of how money grows and wealth is created.

Fortunately, there is a fairly precise form and structure to the growth of money. Money growth, in a sense, is organic. That is, money grows much like apples or corn or flowers or trees. Accordingly, Warren Buffett and Charlie Munger both use the term *seed money* when describing the initial stages of money growth. Then there is time. All things that grow usually depend on seasons that measure intervals of time. Money, like seeds, matures and grows over many seasons. And, of course, seeds require nurturing and much care. Valuable seeds are seldom just thrown to the wind, but instead are planted in rich soil under the most favorable conditions possible, where a gardener will water and watch over them. Seeds first grow into seedlings and then flowers or plants or trees that all are seed bearing upon maturity. It is exactly the same with the growth of money. Seed money that is carefully planted and watched over often bears an abundance of fruit—namely, dividends and capital appreciation—over many seasons. "Money," wrote Benjamin Franklin, "can beget money, and its offspring can beget more." Such is the form and structure of wealth creation. Money growth is really not difficult to understand once one examines the form and structure of how things grow in nature.

People are generally impressed with the word *millionaire*. A millionaire signifies, for many, an image of someone who has made it. Millionaires are successful. Millionaires have money. Millionaires, in short, have accomplished something very worthwhile and significant. Most people, it seems, would like very much to someday have a million dollars in retirement savings. It perhaps then makes sense to discern the form and structure of money growth by exploring how one becomes a millionaire.

Warren Buffett once conveyed the following story in one of his annual reports. "When Richard Branson, the wealthy owner of Virgin Atlantic Airways, was asked how to become a millionaire, he had a quick answer: 'There's really nothing to it. Start as a billionaire and then buy an airline.'"[2] Starting with $1 billion and then losing $999 million is no doubt very doable when taking a top-down approach to saving and investing. Most investors, however, must start from nothing and then figure out a way to move upward in net worth.

When establishing form and structure to a process, it makes sense to tackle that difficult problem by first establishing the most direct route to the answer. For example, what is the easiest way to become a millionaire when starting from the bottom up? Finding a repeatable method that gives a person the least expensive way to become a millionaire and that has the highest probability of success, is an excellent route to discover structure to this difficult process. That is the point raised in the question: How does one become a millionaire? The answer is found in discovering the basic pattern that best explains the process of individual wealth creation.

The perfect picture of wealth creation is a very easy story to understand. A single money seed carefully planted at birth can yield as many as 100 additional money seeds over the many seasons of a person's early years and working lifetime. Money growth mirrors nearly precisely the pattern of natural growth. Few things happen in the process of wealth creation that do not also occur when one plants an acorn or kernel of corn or cantaloupe seed. Seeds, soil, seasons, and sunshine produce more seeds. Just as cantaloupe seeds produce more cantaloupes, seed money, when invested wisely, produces more money.

One of the easiest ways to make a millionaire is for someone to give a newborn $10,000 at birth and then invest that seed money into the soil of a reputable mutual fund. By retirement age, the $10,000 seed will have grown like a tree over many seasons to $1 million.[3] A caretaker gives the infant $10,000 and plants that seed money in stocks, and the market piles up $990,000 in earnings over that person's lifetime. All the infant has to do is just simply grow old and refrain from ever touching the money until retirement age. It is a near-foolproof way of becoming a millionaire.

There are some obvious contingencies, however, to all this easy money that results in the first million dollars. First, the generous gift depends on having someone around at birth who is kind, wise, and wealthy—and willing to fork over a healthy stash of dough. Discovering such a person is indeed one major contingency. Then there is this whole matter of stock market returns. Forecasting market returns 66 years into the future must come with some sort of qualification. It is assumed, for example, that in this particular illustration that the stock market will return 7.2 percent a year on average. This, of course, is not a uniform or linear return. Some years will have stellar performance, and other years are likely to be dismal. The market should be able to generate average annual returns of somewhere around 7 percent, nonetheless, as long as the U.S. economy continues to grow at a rate of between 2 and 4 percent annually. Investing in a diversified mutual fund is really nothing more than making an investment in American business. Stock market valuations grow as companies grow. An annual stock market growth rate of 7.2 percent is a reasonable assumption as long as the economy grows by 3.2 percent, inflation averages 2 percent, and dividends pay 2 percent.[4] Sometimes people will advise investors to expect returns higher than 7.2 percent. Caution is in order. The market can, and perhaps will, do much better than 7.2 percent over the next 66 years. Make certain, however, that you understand fully the assumptions supporting any projected investment returns higher than 7.2 percent. And don't forget, it is possible that markets as well as diversified mutual funds can disappoint and fail to achieve long-term growth rates as high as 7.2 percent. It is only an estimate, based on what are believed to be reasonable assumptions.

It is helpful to graph a picture when visualizing how $10,000 grows into $1 million (see Figure 4-1). Start by writing $10,000 in the far left bottom corner. Move out 10 years and then double the $10,000. At age 10, therefore, the account will have grown to $20,000. Ten years later, the $20,000 will double again to $40,000. This pattern will continue throughout one's lifetime. A decade under these circumstances is much like a growing season. Money doubles in value every decade or every

FIGURE 4-1 *Money Growth Curve*

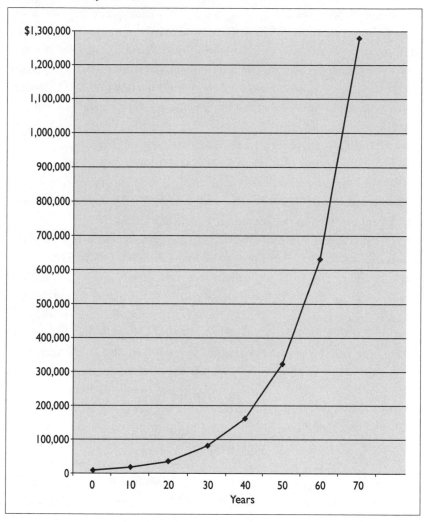

season when the average annual return is 7.2 percent. A person who starts with $10,000 at birth will have approximately $40,000 at age 20, $80,000 at age 30, $160,000 at age 40, $320,000 at age 50, $640,000 at age 60, and $1 million by age 66. If the stock market averages better than 7.2 percent, the investor will have more than $1 million at retirement, and likewise, if the return is less than 7.2 percent, the investor will have less than $1 million.

Money growth is understood by many investors to be the result of the magic of compounding. It indeed is astonishing to watch $640,000 grow by more than $300,000 within just six years. That is why it is helpful to draw a picture of $10,000 growing into $1 million over a lifetime. As can be clearly seen, there is little that is mysterious about compounding. It is nothing more than the rate at which money grows. Mathematically, nothing happened for the investor at age 60 that did not happen at birth. Money doubles every decade when the average return is 7.2 percent. One dollar doubling into $2, from a purely mathematical perspective, is no more remarkable than $500,000 doubling into $1 million. The key is not so much found in compounding, but rather in putting together a sizable sum of money that can double for the investor. Without significant savings, money cannot grow significantly.

The picture of $10,000 in savings growing to $1 million serves several useful purposes. By following the line from $10,000 to $1,000,000, you can determine approximately where you should be on the road to wealth creation should you wish to become a millionaire by retirement age. For example, a 33-year-old can look at this picture and see that she should have $100,000 already saved should she wish to retire with $1 million. If she has more than $100,000 saved, then she is ahead of the curve, and if she has less than $100,000 saved, she is behind the curve. She is completely off the track if nothing has been put away yet for retirement. Most workers, because they did not receive $10,000 at birth, will likely discover that when it comes to building a $1 million nest egg for retirement, they are behind the curve.

Saving, actually, is not so much a matter of getting ahead, but rather catching up. The proper mental image or picture clearly reveals that the clock starts ticking at birth. Time, the world's most valuable commodity, begins to slowly slip away on day one. Unless one enters this world with the necessary seed money for retirement already provided, that person gets further and further behind with each passing day if he or she does not save. This particular understanding of form and structure not only illustrates the process of wealth creation over time, but also defines the worker's role in the process as well. Those born without seed money must start now and save aggressively to catch up. That is why the old gardener, when asked about the best time to plant a tree, responded by saying "30 years ago."

Drawing a picture of $10,000 growing to $1 million poignantly underscores the reality of catching up. A child who dreams of becoming a millionaire, but starts life with zero net worth, is $20,000 in the hole by age 10. Likewise, a college graduate who aspires to become a millionaire starts work $40,000 behind the eight ball. People sometimes believe the clock begins ticking whenever they decide to start saving or land their first job. They are wrong. The clock has been diligently grinding away since the very first moment of breath. Seasons progress through time barren, whenever there is an absence of seed money.

It is truly amazing, when pausing to reflect upon the early lives of Benjamin Franklin, Charlie Munger, and Warren Buffett, how they were each able to figure out critical aspects of wealth creation at such a young age. None received generous handouts in the form of seed money at birth. Buffett's dad was busted by the Depression within a year of Buffett's birth, and Franklin's dad was trying to keep up with the expenses of rearing 14 children. Each of these three individuals, nonetheless, seemed to intuitively sense that they, even as teenagers, were already behind in their savings. The clock was ticking; it was as though these men realized that precious money-growing seasons were passing by without the possibility for any real money growth because of insufficient seed money. Once aware of their situation, each began working and saving aggressively. These men demonstrated an uncanny understanding of wealth creation.

Once seasons begin to pass, it is very difficult to catch up. The tough news is that it requires a tremendous amount of focus and determination to catch up financially. It is not impossible, but it is difficult. It demands hard work. But there is good news, too. Once investors start to make some tangible progress on the road to wealth creation, they seldom give up and abandon ship. Unlike dieting where one must battle to merely maintain reduced weight, those who work to save and invest get to see their money grow and grow. Consequently, people generally do not start from zero, then get to $120,000 in savings, and all of a sudden say, "Wealth creation is not for me. I'm throwing in the towel." Early on, some are tempted to quit and indeed do jump ship. But once the process starts to bear fruit, investors tend to stay on track. Becoming financially independent is an extremely rewarding and meaningful experience. Wealth creation tempers individuals over time with discipline and patience. Hard-earned wealth often changes a person's perspective on life as that person experiences a greater sense of freedom and independence and security. The growth of money provides stability.

The process for becoming wealthy or financially independent through savings follows the exact same form and structure as the $10,000 gift at birth, which grows all the way to $1 million by retirement age. Wealth creation, for most, starts with seed money, or savings. This seed money will yield predictable amounts of growth in dollars over a season. Again, a 7.2 percent average annual return will result in the money doubling every decade. As we know, if an investor wishes to have $1 million by age 66, then the easiest path for that person is to start life with $10,000 in seed money. Those born without such a generous handout must start saving now, because the theoretical seed money is on a track that is doubling every decade. Once money starts to grow, it is like a tree spreading roots, so catching up is a major project. For example, $10,000 compounding by 7.2 percent will grow by $320,000 in the sixth decade and $640,000 in the seventh decade. *Those wishing to become wealthy must track the rate at which theoretical seed money grows and then implement a savings plan to catch up to those numbers by retirement age.* Money growth is not magic. It is not luck. The form and structure of money growth is primarily a natural phenomenon. It requires seeds (savings), seasons (time), nutrition (investments), and nurturing. There is nothing mysterious or foreign or complicated about it.

The Three Questions of Success

Accomplishing any difficult task in life requires answering three questions:

What is my goal?
How do I measure my progress?
What must I do now to reach my goal?

Success depends on finding answers to these three questions. Accomplishing financial independence is no different.

Take, for example, a student who wishes to run the mile race in under 5 minutes by the first meet of the track season. The goal is clearly defined: running a mile in under 5 minutes. The student can measure progress by running four laps around the track at a pace of 75 seconds per lap. Assume the first and final laps are under 75 seconds, but the second and third laps are well over 75 seconds. The runner will therefore need to build endurance, increase lung capacity, and strengthen leg muscles. The runner must run longer distances in practice to increase endurance, run sprints to enhance lung capacity, and practice six days a week to strengthen leg muscles. As quarter lap times improve, the runner gains confidence as she or he approaches the stated goal. A well-designed training program for athletes acknowledges the three questions of success.

A worker who wishes to get a promotion is another valid example. The worker must first set a goal by identifying the position that he or she seeks. Next, the worker must list all the qualifications for such a position. The worker will then proceed with an action plan to meet the required qualifications. The worker can measure progress by completing those necessary qualifications such as additional education or job experience. A determined worker will also likely want to go beyond the completion of necessary qualifications by volunteering for extra assignments, working overtime, and sponsoring new initiatives. Engaging supervisors in the promotion process is usually vital to enhancing one's career path. Supervisors will generally offer insight as to those next steps that must be accomplished before one is ready for a key promotion. People who move ahead in business learn how to set goals, measure their progress, and clearly define next steps.

One of the most visible and aggressive implementations of these three questions took place in May of 1961. President John F. Kennedy, when addressing the Congress, said: "I believe this nation should commit itself to achieving the goal, before this decade is out, of landing a man on the moon and returning him safely to earth." The goal, landing a man on the moon, was clearly stated. The timetable was also explicit. There were eight years and seven months to get the job done. The next step, although not articulated, was obvious. America first had to get a person to orbit the earth. A month earlier, a Soviet cosmonaut had been the first person to orbit the planet. The United States was very much behind in the space race. We as a nation had to catch up.

The world watched as the United States measured progress. John Glenn orbited the earth three times in early 1962. The next step was Gemini wherein two men were launched together into space. The Apollo program followed as three men traveled together in space. One Christmas Eve astronaut Bill Anders and two others circled the moon. The entire world watched and measured our progress with this challenging endeavor as one necessary step followed the other. Finally, on July 20, 1969, the seemingly impossible task neared completion as Neil Armstrong landed on the moon with these words. "That's one small step for man, one giant leap for mankind." There were 5 months and 11 days to spare in the decade. The free world celebrated.

Retirement planning is much like going to the moon. It demands an easy-to-understand goal and timetable, stringent measurement, and clearly defined next steps. Those who cannot articulate their goal, accurately measure progress, or understand necessary next steps are just as likely to wind up on the moon as they are to ever become financially independent. Their chances of retiring wealthy, in other words, are basically nil. Wealth, as emphasized earlier, is a self-controlled process. The attainment of financial independence favors strongly those who prepare. As 45 million Americans participate in 401(k) retirement savings programs, it is eerie to think the overwhelming majority of these workers have no way to accurately declare personal retirement goals, institute viable methods for measuring their saving and investment progress, and define necessary next steps. Walk down any corridor in any company in any city and ask any employee who participates in a 401(k) plan these three basic questions: How much money do you need to retire? Are you ahead or behind the curve, and by how much? What must you do now? Very few workers have the answers to these elementary questions of wealth creation. Those without the answers to these three questions are left in the hands of luck and chance. Great things in life are seldom accomplished by luck.

It is much harder for nations to get to the moon than for individuals to become financially independent. Only one nation has ever been to the moon, whereas millions and millions of individuals have become financially independent. Ordinary individuals, in every single generation of American history, have figured out how to become wealthy. The process is very much the same as America followed in the 1960s in overcoming unbelievable odds to find a way to the moon. It starts with finding the answers to those three questions that define success.

Looking Ahead

The next three chapters build on the form and structure of individual wealth creation by finding specific answers to the three questions of success. Chapter 5 teaches readers to define their retirement savings goal. In Chapter 6 readers discover how to measure their savings and how to determine the future value of their current savings. Chapter 7 covers those next steps—or what precisely one must start saving now to become financially independent by retirement age.

There are a total of five steps necessary for computing the answer to the three questions of success. Because salaries are paid in dollars and cents, there is arithmetic involved in each of these steps. The math, however, is not at all complicated. It is simple multiplication, division, addition, and subtraction. So, don't worry about the math. You'll get it.

You will want to remain mindful that the aim of this book concerns the attainment of personal financial independence at age 67. This, as I am sure you are aware, is an ambitious goal. Do not let the numbers, especially as they relate to your personal situation, surprise or discourage you. The goals, measurements, and next steps may initially appear out of your reach. Don't panic. Stay with the material. Later we'll discuss strategies for getting on track.

It is highly unlikely, as you well know, for any two workers to share identical numbers when planning for retirement. Each person's financial circumstances are unique. Travel through any neighborhood or down any assembly line, and, even though wages and benefits may be close to identical, you'll discover personal savings rates and monies put away vary widely. It is for these reasons the book will now turn inward, away from the general retirement landscape, to identifying and addressing your own wealth objectives.

Three simple charts and five easy steps are all it takes to establish your retirement destination, review where you are presently, and define your next steps. That is the beauty of working with numbers. The form and structure of wealth creation clearly outlines the path to financial independence. We shall now identify the path to financial independence that has your name on it.

CHAPTER 5

Setting a Personal Retirement Goal

Steps 1 and 2

You've got to be old with money because to be old without it is just too awful.
Tennessee Williams

Those who are financially independent are able to live for the rest of their days without ever again receiving a paycheck. That essentially is what it means to be retired: no more paychecks. Further, those who are financially independent are able to live the remainder of their lives without ever having to worry about running out of money or having their standard of living diminished.

Setting goals is fundamental to human life. Goals, in a very real sense, are one of the primary characteristics that distinguish human beings from all other animals. Although animals are amazing creatures with all kinds of remarkable features and personalities, they do very little in the way of planning. Animals basically exist on a day-to-day basis, whereas humans are able to pursue a certain direction or purpose in life. In fact, most people are largely defined and shaped by their private and professional goals.

It is inconceivable, for instance, to imagine a physician performing surgery with no idea as to whether the patient is in need of an appendectomy or tonsillectomy. Likewise, it is laughable to conceive of two commercial airline pilots having no idea where in the world they are destined as the jetliner gets towed away from the gate. The absence of goals is an absolute absurdity to the rational human mind. It is for this reason police officers, when pulling over motorists, will often ask, "Where are you headed?" Those who cannot articulate a clear destination are often headed for trouble.

The purpose of a 401(k) retirement plan is to make workers wealthy by retirement age. Those who participate in these saving and investing vehicles should expect their 401(k) account balances to be their single largest asset by retirement age. Many, if not most, participants should plan to someday have $1 million in their 401(k) plans. The goal of those who participate seriously in these saving plans is personal financial independence.

It is very easy for workers to establish their personal retirement savings goal. All they have to do is find their age on Figure 5-1.[1]

Next to each age is a four-digit number. Multiply this four-digit number by your annual salary or wage. The product or answer is your personal retirement savings goal at age 67 (the retirement age for Americans born after 1959, based on Social Security tables).

It works best to start with an example. Let's assume a worker is 31 years old and earns $30,640 annually. On Figure 5-1, next to age 31 is the four-digit number 32.64. To find their personal retirement savings goal, multiply 32.64 times the annual salary of $30,640 (32.64 × $30,640 = $1,000,090). The answer, or retirement goal, is $1,000,090.

Some workers may want to plan for a retirement income that is less than their current annual salaries. For example, a worker might be currently earning $120,000 a year, but may want to plan for a retirement income of $80,000. The worker figures that at age 67 all her major expenses will be gone. For example, college for the children will have been paid in full and the mortgage retired. Whenever people can identify a particular dollar amount of annual income for retirement, then all they have to do is multiply that dollar amount by 20. For example, if someone is certain they will need an annual income of $80,000 in retirement, they just multiply $80,000 × 20. The goal in this case will be $1.6 million.

When planning for retirement, one must be certain to include provisions for inflation. Inflation is a silent thief that literally robs the retired and the unprepared. Often, when retired people return to work after staying home for ten years because they can no longer make ends meet, the culprit is inflation. Inflation, in short, is an increase in the price of goods and services. Inflation averages around 2 percent a year.

FIGURE 5-1 *Setting Personal Retirement Goals*

Age	Factor	Age	Factor	Age	Factor
18	42.22	35	30.15	52	21.53
19	41.39	36	29.56	53	21.11
20	40.58	37	28.98	54	20.70
21	39.79	38	28.41	55	20.29
22	39.01	39	27.86	56	19.89
23	38.24	40	27.31	57	19.50
24	37.49	41	26.77	58	19.12
25	36.76	42	26.25	59	18.75
26	36.04	43	25.73	60	18.38
27	35.33	44	25.23	61	18.02
28	34.64	45	24.74	62	17.67
29	33.96	46	24.25	63	17.32
30	33.29	47	23.78	64	16.98
31	32.64	48	23.31	65	16.65
32	32.00	49	22.85	66	16.32
33	31.37	50	22.40		
34	30.76	51	21.96		

STEP 1:   Setting a Personal Retirement Goal

Retirement goal = Salary × Age factor (Figure 5-1)

Example: Participant is 31 years old, earns $30,640, and has saved $12,500.

1. Find age 31 on Figure 5-1. The age factor is 32.64

2. Plug the numbers into the formula.
   Retirement goal = Salary × Age factor
   $1,000,090 = $30,640 × 32.64

   The retirement goal for this 31-year-old worker is $1,000,090.

A 50-year old who lives comfortably on $50,000 today, will likely need $100,000 at age 85 to maintain a similar lifestyle. Inflation in the near term is barely noticeable. Over longer periods, however, inflation is a genuine bandit. Prices in a vibrant economy have a tendency to move upward. Dollars, over time, generally buy less and less. It is for this reason the factors for determining personal retirement goals in Figure 5-1 have been adjusted to account for inflation.

The primary aim of financial independence is for workers to live the rest of their lives without running out of money or compromising their standard of living. Saving and investing apart from a well-defined future financial goal are nothing more than shooting in the dark or horsing around with guessing games. Human beings, as mentioned earlier, are largely defined by their goals in life. Those whose goals are ill-defined are almost certain to come up short at retirement. Running out of money at any age, but especially in old age, is an unthinkable nightmare. Playwright Tennessee Williams underscored this reality perfectly in *Cat on a Hot Tin Roof* when Margaret cried, "You've got to be old with money because to be old without it is just too awful."[2] It is for this reason that all employees who participate in 401(k) retirement plans at work should know how much money they will need to retire at age 67. Workers, if ever asked how much money they need to retire, should never have to suffer embarrassment from not knowing the answer to such a fundamental question. Companies sponsoring 401(k) plans for workers, as well as those financial institutions providing the investments, should make sure all plan participants are able to confidently articulate their retirement goals.

Overcoming *Can't*

Chief among the primary reasons people fail to become wealthy is belief in the word *can't*. When they first see the amount of money required for the attainment of financial independence at retirement age, workers often get caught off guard. This abrupt surprise sometimes overwhelms them. It often triggers a negative response, such as "I can't do this."

Unfortunately, one of the most reliable indicators of future results is the word *can't*. Whenever a person sincerely believes something can't get done, that belief invariably becomes a self-fulfilling prophecy. Few words predict failure with such astounding accuracy as can't. Can't is one possible reason there are so many families with insufficient retirement savings. Can't concedes defeat and throws in the towel before the game even starts. Whenever one submits to can't, failure is almost always a certainty.

Can't usually reveals either an inability or unwillingness to assess human potential. It is natural for people to look at the numbers on their paycheck and just see limits. This book, however, seeks to open a whole new world of possibilities for those numbers stamped on each paycheck. Your goal at retirement is based on your current income. There is a direct correlation between financial independence and what you are now earning. Money, when saved from each paycheck and invested wisely, has the potential to grow. Can't, when viewed from this context, is really nothing more than a verbal admission that one is experiencing difficulty assessing the possibilities of money growth.

It is easy to understand why any person would respond by saying "can't" when confronted suddenly with an unexpected or extremely difficult task or responsibility. Certain goals are extremely challenging. Questioning one's ability when assessing extraordinarily difficult circumstances is normal. For example, it is one thing to discuss financial independence. Wealth, after all, is an interesting ideal. It is quite another matter, however, to learn for the first time that one must go from zero net worth to $1 million on an annual income of $35,000. "I can't:" is a very typical response for the worker who hears that news for the first time. Can't, nonetheless, must never be the final word.

There are myriad resources supporting the process of wealth creation for workers who participate in 401(k) retirement plans. First, a 401(k) plan provides workers with a painless way to save for retirement. Future retirement obligations are deducted from each paycheck and invested. The process is referred to as painless because workers are generally able to spend all that remains in their paychecks once retirement savings have been met. Second, personal retirement contributions are not taxed, unless they instead select a Roth option, in which case the earnings on any contributions are not taxed at retirement. In any event, the Internal Revenue Service (IRS) subsidizes personal retirement savings whenever money is deposited into a 401(k). Third, the earnings are tax deferred until one withdraws the money at retirement. Deferring taxes until retirement significantly increases the value of retirement dollars at retirement. Fourth, companies will sometimes match employee retirement contributions. A common matching formula allocates an

additional 0.50¢ for every $1 a worker contributes into his or her ac-
count. For example, if a worker puts $1,000 into the 401(k) account, the
company would match the contribution by $500. The result is an imme-
diate return of 50 percent. Some refer to matching as free money. (Most
matching contributions are capped at 3 percent of one's total compen-
sation. For instance, a person earning $30,000 could be eligible to re-
ceive up to $900, or 3 percent of annual compensation. Also, matching
contributions are often subject to a vesting schedule, which means an
employee must remain at a company for a certain number of years, generally six, before all the money contributed by the company belongs to
them.) Finally, mutual fund investments in a 401(k) plan are often priced
on a net asset value (NAV) basis, which means participants are charged
lower fees.

Many companies work with financial professionals. This means the
company-sponsored 401(k) plan comes with the expertise of experienced professionals. One theme appearing throughout this book is the
importance of working with a financial professional. Workers with access to financial professionals have an additional resource vital to the
achievement of reaching aggressive retirement goals.

Retirement goals need not intimidate or overwhelm investors. Worthy goals pull people forward in positive directions. Aggressive goals
often challenge people to look inward and draw from resources such as
determination and creativity that reside deep within the human will.
Difficult-to-achieve goals—retirement or otherwise—provide humans
with some of their finest hours and most memorable moments. Good
almost always results when worthy goals are pursued.

The Ultimate Aim of Wealth

Setting a retirement goal is straightforward. What an investor is really trying to do is replace his or her job. The goal for financial independence is therefore to attain enough money to create earnings each year
equal to the worker's salary or standard of living at retirement. This
amount is approximately the desired annual income multiplied by the
four-digit number that corresponds to one's current age. Drawing from
the earlier example, $1,000,090 will give the 31-year-old, now earning
$30,640, an income of $50,000 at age 67. The increase from $30,640 in

wages to a retirement income of $50,000 factors in the anticipated impact of inflation. A 31-year-old worker currently earning $30,640 and saving for retirement will therefore need about $50,000 at age 67 to maintain the present standard of living due to inflation. Those who achieve financial independence can then expect to live on $1/20$, or 5 percent, of their retirement nest egg.

It is important when preparing for retirement to understand the significance of living on just 5 percent of one's retirement nest egg each year. Withdrawing more than 5 percent could cause the investor to eventually run out of money. Financial independence is defined by maintaining one's standard of living for as long as one is alive without ever having to worry about running out of money. To ensure that one always remains wealthy, withdrawals should remain limited to no more than 5 percent.

When a person is accumulating wealth, one's retirement investment portfolio receives money from numerous sources. Most employees will contribute money from their paycheck up until their final day of work. Further, employees eligible to receive profit-sharing, pension, or 401(k) matches from their employer, will receive additional contributions to their retirement nest egg. Finally, there are the earnings growth, dividends, and interest payments that come from the investments. As stated earlier, investors can expect average annual investment returns of 7.2 percent. When a person finally retires, he or she often fully depend on earnings growth, dividends, and interest payments as the sole contributors to their portfolio.

When retired, it is not unreasonable to expect a well-balanced and diversified portfolio to produce average annual returns in the neighborhood of 7 percent. The investor can withdraw the 2 percent that represents income from dividends and 3 percent that represents growth in the economy. The remaining 2.2 percent should get plowed back into the retirement portfolio. Putting 2.2 percent of total earnings growth back into the portfolio will protect the investor from the negative effects of inflation. Unless one continually reinvests approximately 2 percent of each year's earnings, the principal value of one's portfolio will likely erode away over time. Those who spend everything they make in retirement could eventually run out of money or have their standard of living diminished, unless, of course, they die first.[3]

Asset allocation, although always important, is exceedingly crucial when one is retired. Ideally, once retired, investors should try to structure their portfolios with the help of a financial professional, so that cash flow (namely, dividends and interest payments) meets the 5 percent spending requirements. One should try to avoid, at least in my judgment, withdrawing principal when retired. Live on the cash flow of 5 percent and then reinvest any excess income or earnings back into the portfolio.[4]

There are currently several retirement models that recommend investors to only withdraw 4 percent of their nest egg each year. These models are even more conservative than my recommendation of 5 percent. Any withdrawal rate less than 5 percent is perfectly acceptable, although it may increase the amount of money one needs to retire financially independent or slightly reduce one's standard of living in retirement. When the alternative is running out of money, it is always best to err on the side of caution and capital preservation.

STEP 2:   Defining Income at Age 67

Income at age 67 = Retirement goal × 0.05 (from Step 1)

Example: Participant is 31 years old, earns $30,640, and has saved $12,500.

1. Determine retirement goal from Step 1.

2. Multiply retirement goal by 0.05.
   Income at 67 = Retirement goal × 0.05
   $50,000 = $1,000,090 × 0.05

   The income at age 67 for this 31-year-old is $50,000.
   ($50,000 is rounded down from $50,004.50)

CHAPTER 6

Measuring Savings Progress

Steps 3 and 4

The first principle is to not fool yourself, and you are the easiest person to fool.
Richard Feynman

Millions of Americans have been saving and investing in 401(k) plans, 403(b) programs, 457 plans, and IRAs for many years. At the end of 2004, the average participant's 401(k) account balance was approximately $60,000. Surprisingly, when surveyed, a fairly high percentage of 401(k) participants were reasonably confident of their ability to achieve their personal retirement savings goal. Workers in these surveys seldom appear distressed or alarmed about future retirement shortfalls. These surveys, however, typically measure only personal opinion. Workers are seldom, if ever, asked to explain how they are able to quantify their impressions.

There are many ways to view the $60,000 account balances in personal retirement accounts. First, let's observe what $60,000 will buy in today's dollars. Daily newspapers are often stuffed with circular advertisements. Looking at the wide array of consumer items on sale in the newspaper, there is hardly anything $60,000 will not buy: $60,000 will pay for a cruise to most anywhere in the world, a Mercedes Benz E Class sedan, or even a motor home; $60,000 will fill your closets with clothes and your family room with a widescreen high-definition television set that includes surround sound; $60,000 will pay for several trips to Disney World or even four years of college at many state universities. When measured by what $60,000 will buy in today's dollars, at least in terms of what the newspapers advertise, these 401(k) account balances contain a lot of money.

When viewed from the perspective of retirement or financial independence, however, the present value of $60,000 plays an entirely different role. The chief aim of retirement savings is to replace one's employer. Workers can be financially independent only when they can continue at their current standard of living without receiving another paycheck. When measured from the perspective of replacing one's employer, $60,000 is a woefully insignificant sum unless the worker is quite young and this money has a long time to grow. It takes 20 times one's income at retirement to replace a person's job. Thus, $60,000 produces only about $8.25 a day in retirement income, which is why it is imperative to be able to accurately measure one's progress when saving and investing for retirement.

Any time individuals are without the proper tools for measurement and verification, they are left to create their own perception of reality. This is why so many stories told by recreational fishermen are light-heartedly suspect. A three-pound smallmouth bass can easily become an eight-pound pike when there are no scales for measurement readily available. It is all a matter of perception. Listening to fish stories is so entertaining for this reason. There are hardly any limits to all the exaggeration. It is a world of make-believe wherein perceptions of reality are easily stretched to mythological proportions.

It is funny, in a peculiar sort of way, how little measurement actually gets done in our day-to-day lives. Hardly anyone measures the volume of air it takes to breathe or calories essential for proper nutrition. We tease ourselves when dieting into thinking all we had was a little harmless afternoon snack, when in fact half a cake was consumed. "The first principle," wrote Richard Feynman, the famous physicist and late Nobel laureate, "is to not fool yourself, and you are the easiest person to fool."[1] Almost anything is believable whenever someone is unrestrained from measurement and hence left to create his or her own conclusions.

It happens all the time in 401(k) savings programs. Workers sign up and they start saving for retirement. They see some money growth when the monthly and quarterly statements are delivered. People have the perception they are perfectly "on track" with their retirement savings. It is their impression they are getting ahead. After all, there is $60,000 in the account. And 60 grand, so the thinking goes, will buy almost anything.

This, in short, is the great and very real dilemma facing the multitude of employees in company-sponsored 401(k) plans. Participants are without the means to measure savings progress. It is therefore extremely difficult to separate myth from reality when it comes to retirement savings. Saving for retirement is a big-ticket item. Everybody knows that when saving for a big-ticket item, serious amounts of money must be put away. It is a myth to believe workers can adequately get started saving for retirement by putting away only nominal sums of money. It is a myth to believe that if your savings equals the national average or what everyone else seems to have saved, you'll be just fine. It is a myth to believe participants can compensate for years of not saving sufficient sums by getting incredible stock market returns. It is dangerous to believe that bureaucrats and politicians will never lower Social Security benefits or increase the age for retirement within your working lifetime. Those without the means to measurement are left to their impressions.

Measurement liberates the worker from misconception. Measurement separates reality from perception. Measurement produces accountability; it facilitates ownership. Measurement obliterates myth. Measurement lies at the very heart of financial independence. Those who measure with reliable instruments can rest peacefully at night. They have the assurance of being on the right track. Measurement precludes bias. Measurement is trustworthy; it is grounded in facts. Measurement delivers a clear, crisp, concise accounting of not only where one has been, but also where one is headed.

Retirement is made possible when workers attain definable numbers measured in dollars. Retirement goals are very easy to measure. There is no need for any worker to ever get surprised upon approaching retirement age. Workers should grow accustomed to measuring their retirement progress at least once annually throughout the entirety of their working years. Every pay raise or bonus or cost of living increase affects a worker's standard of living not only in present terms, but in retirement terms as well. The truth of the matter is, workers journey each day on the road to retirement. Remaining abreast of one's progress only makes sense for the serious traveler.

Once one grows comfortable measuring retirement progress, myths and inaccurate perceptions become readily identifiable. Nonsense no longer masquerades as wisdom. Broad generalities, when pronounced without any numerical quantification whatsoever, are held suspect. The ability to measure equips one with knowledge and confidence as concrete numbers provide clear direction.

All one has to do when measuring retirement savings progress is find the four-digit number next to one's age (see Figure 6-1, column A)[2] and

FIGURE 6-1 *Measuring Personal Retirement Savings*

Age	Column A	Age	Column A	Age	Column A	Age	Column A
0	0.0095	17	0.0309	34	0.1008	51	0.3288
1	0.0102	18	0.0331	35	0.1081	52	0.3524
2	0.0109	19	0.0355	36	0.1159	53	0.3778
3	0.0117	20	0.0381	37	0.1242	54	0.4050
4	0.0125	21	0.0408	38	0.1332	55	0.4342
5	0.0134	22	0.0438	39	0.1427	56	0.4654
6	0.0144	23	0.0469	40	0.1530	57	0.4989
7	0.0154	24	0.0503	41	0.1640	58	0.5349
8	0.0165	25	0.0539	42	0.1758	59	0.5734
9	0.0177	26	0.0578	43	0.1885	60	0.6147
10	0.0190	27	0.0620	44	0.2021	61	0.6589
11	0.0204	28	0.0664	45	0.2166	62	0.7064
12	0.0218	29	0.0712	46	0.2322	63	0.7572
13	0.0234	30	0.0763	47	0.2489	64	0.8117
14	0.0251	31	0.0818	48	0.2669	65	0.8702
15	0.0269	32	0.0877	49	0.2861	66	0.9328
16	0.0288	33	0.0941	50	0.3067	67	1.0000

STEP 3: Measuring Progress

On-track measurement = Retirement goal × Column A factor
                         (from Step 1)   (from Figure 6-1)

Example: Participant is 31 years old, earns $30,640, and has saved $12,500.

1. Find age 31 in Figure 6-1. The Column A factor is 0.0818.

2. Plug the numbers into the formula.
   On-track measurement = Retirement goal × Column A factor
   $81,800 = $1,000,090 × 0.0818

The participant needs $81,800 to be "on track" with retirement savings. Because the participant has only $12,500 saved, the participant is behind the curve.

($81,000 is rounded down from $81,807)

multiply by the retirement goal. That's all there is to it. It is one simple multiplication exercise. Using the same example initiated in Chapter 5 resulted in a retirement goal of $1,000,090. When the retirement goal is multiplied by 0.0818 (the number next to age 31), we find that the worker should have $81,800 already in savings.[3] The worker in our example, with $12,500 in savings, is behind the curve.

The $60,000 Question

This chapter opened with an observation that the average 401(k) account balance is $60,000. We learned that $60,000 is indeed a lot of money when viewed in terms of what it can purchase. From a retirement perspective, however, it is apparent that $60,000 provides little in the way of lifetime income. It is largely insufficient as a final nest egg for most workers.

There is also a third perspective from which to view $60,000. What will $60,000 likely be worth at retirement age? This is a question of significant importance, for how can a person adequately plan for retirement unless one is able to easily calculate the future value of the money already saved? Having the ability to look through the windshield of time is vital when mapping a viable course for retirement. Hence the importance of knowing the answer to the $60,000 question: What will my savings likely be worth when I retire?

When we draw from memories of the past, our minds do not usually capture entire days or hours or even full minutes. Whenever we recall something from the past, it is often packaged in a moment. And as we look back in life, we typically remember only the most extreme moments of our existence. Those times that were either the very best or the very worst, as the novelist Charles Dickens once put it. The mediocre or the ordinary or the day-to-day seems to quietly get swept away and buried within our minds. We retain, in a sense, no insignificant memories.

It is from this perspective that what could have become an otherwise typical or ordinary day from almost 20 years ago has become one of the more significant events in my lifetime. Bonnie and I were trying as hard as we could to save as much as possible, but we were up against some stiff headwinds. She was home taking care of two baby boys (loss of her income). The boys were in diapers (we thought diapers would be cheaper than disposables—big mistake!). We had just moved to Chicago (the rent had tripled). I was trying to get a new sales territory off the ground (tons of rejection, few sales). One day, out of the blue, my boss called to say there was a $5,000 bonus check in the mail.

This was just unbelievably good news. It was truly a lucky break. But, with babies running around in diapers, rent that had recently tripled, and college loans still outstanding, five grand can quickly vanish. We carefully studied all our options. Then we asked ourselves an important question and made a critical calculation: How much would $5,000 be worth to us when we were ready to retire? The answer was $50,000. The discovery that the bonus check would take $50,000 off our retirement goal, and our decision to save the full amount marked a meaningful turning point in our lives. None of our current needs and desires could match the impact of $50,000 in future savings. We still talk about the day we walked into the brokerage office and deposited that bonus check.

Finding the answer to the $60,000 question, the future value of your savings, is not at all difficult. Amazingly, most of the work has already been done in Steps 1 and 3. Take your current savings and divide by the on-track measurement from Step 3. Then take this answer, or quotient, and multiply by the retirement goal from Step 1. To continue with the hypothetical worker example already in place, you divide the worker's current savings of $12,500 by $81,800 (on-track measurement). The answer or quotient is 0.1528. Now multiply 0.1528 by the retirement goal of $1,000,090. Thus, $12,500, for the hypothetical worker in this example, should be worth around $152,800 when that participant reaches age 67.

As these examples indicate, this important calculation will be useful on numerous occasions throughout your working lifetime. Not only is it a handy way to calculate the future value of savings, but also the future value of bonuses, possible inheritances or gifts, as well as certain capital gains resulting from the sale of property or securities. Money, as you know, especially unexpected financial windfalls, can quickly vanish. Knowing how to make future calculations gives you the tools to look through the windshield of time. Present needs and priorities will often appear trivial when measured against future dollars. Yes, $60,000 will buy a lot of things for a 34-year-old worker. Most of these things, however, pale when viewed from the perspective of the $600,000 it can equal at age 67, which is why Step 4 is so very important. It puts to rest the $60,000 question.

STEP 4: Determining the Future Value of Current Savings

Future value quotient = Current savings ÷ On-track measurement
(from Step 3)

Future value of current savings = Retirement goal × Future value quotient
(from Step 1)

Example: Participant is 31 years old, earns $30,640, and has saved $12,500.

1. To find the future value quotient, divide the current savings by the on-track measurement from Step 3.
   Future value quotient = Current savings ÷ On-track measurement
   0.1528 = $12,500 ÷ $81,800

2. To find the future value of savings, multiply the retirement goal by the future value quotient
   Future value of savings = Retirement goal × Future value quotient
   $152,800 = $1,000,090 × 0.1528

   The $12,500 in savings will likely grow to $152,800 by the time the participant reaches age 67.
   ($152,800 is rounded down from $152,813)

CHAPTER 7

The Final Step

Step 5

What I really need is to be clear about what I am to do.
Danish thinker, Soren Kierkegaard

There are three constants that unfailingly produce wealth. When someone starts now, saves sufficient sums, and invests wisely, it is exceedingly probable that person will become financially independent. These three constants obviously worked for Benjamin Franklin, Warren Buffett, and Charlie Munger—and they also will work for you. These constants are time tested and true. The three constants, however, are of little value unless they can be defined or quantified. Obviously, 45 million workers are likely to have 45 million different opinions as to what exactly is meant by saving sufficient sums, as the word *sufficient* is open to a nearly infinite variety of meanings. This chapter will attempt to take 45 million different circumstances and finalize a uniform structure to the whole process of wealth creation by clearly defining what one must save now to become financially independent at retirement.

All across America there are real people with real names and real jobs and real savings. These people go to work each day and save money from every single hour of labor. These workers understand that the burden of providing for their retirement is rapidly shifting to their shoulders. They know the future is coming; they know time will not wait. It is imperative for these workers, should they ever hope to become wealthy, to know what they must save now to become financially independent at retirement age.

A recent poll surveyed some baby boomers, American adults born between 1946 and 1963, and asked about their opinions regarding retirement. "Two-thirds of those surveyed *believe* they are saving at a rate needed to maintain their lifestyle" in retirement.[1] The operative word, of course, is *believe*. Had these same baby boomers been instead asked to define or name the precise rate at which they must save, it would be impressive if even 6 percent had been able to give the right answer.

Workers able to narrow the gap between truth and belief, reality and myth, and quantification and impression will have a tremendous advantage as the country continues progressing toward an ownership society. Those who possess answers to real questions are able to stand above indecision and obfuscation. Knowledge imbues workers with legitimate power, whereas mere belief creates a false sense of security. Those with the currency of knowledge are likely to profit most in an ownership society.

When people are armed with knowledge, they are inclined to make the right choice. The worker on the assembly line, in this regard, stands equal to the executive in the corner suite, when it comes to wealth creation. Personal financial independence is not specific to any position, job skills, or education; numbers and time determine it. Whoever saves the proper amount over the proper amount of years will likely walk into retirement wealthy.

Knowledge, however, is not without limitations. Knowing does not necessarily make one wealthy. The genesis of success is also grounded in action. It is, as the great Danish thinker, Soren Kierkegaard, wrote once in his journal. "What I really need is to be clear about *what I am to do*, not about what I must know."[2] It is precisely the same with personal retirement planning. Those who wish to retire wealthy must be exceedingly clear about what it is they must do. Start now and save sufficient sums as defined by the final step.

The next 401(k) meeting you attend will be far different than all those in the past. You will then know what you want out of your 401(k) program. You will be equipped to take ownership of the process. You can look forward to the future secure in the knowledge that you are taking care of your retirement. You will be clear about what you must do.

The Final Step

The fifth and final step involves identifying the exact amount of money you must save from each paycheck in order to achieve your retirement goal by age 67. There are four parts to the final step. Find the future value quotient from 1 in Step 4 and subtract from 1 (1 – future

STEP 5: Finding the Percent to Be Saved from Every Paycheck

A. Savings quotient = 1 – Future value quotient

B. Savings percent = Savings quotient × Column B factor

C. Annual savings requirement = Savings percent × Income at 67 (Step 2)

D. Percent from each paycheck = Annual savings requirement ÷ Current salary

Example: Participant is 31 years old, earns $30,640, and has saved $12,500.

A. Find savings quotient: 1 – Future value quotient

   0.8472 = 1 – 0.1528

B. Find savings percent: Savings quotient × Column B factor

   0.0995 = 0.8472 × 0.1175

C. Find annual savings payment: Savings percent × Income at age 67

   $4,975 = 0.0995 × $50,000

D. Calculate percentage from each paycheck: Annual savings requirement ÷ Annual salary

   16.24% = $4,975 ÷ $30,640

The participant needs to save 16.24 percent from each paycheck.

FIGURE 7-1 *Savings Goal Requirement*

Age	Column B	Age	Column B	Age	Column B
18	0.0440	35	0.1610	52	0.7441
19	0.0474	36	0.1744	53	0.8315
20	0.0511	37	0.1891	54	0.9335
21	0.0550	38	0.2052	55	1.0538
22	0.0593	39	0.2228	56	1.1974
23	0.0639	40	0.2422	57	1.3714
24	0.0689	41	0.2635	58	1.5859
25	0.0743	42	0.2870	59	1.8560
26	0.0801	43	0.3130	60	2.2058
27	0.0864	44	0.3418	61	2.6748
28	0.0933	45	0.3739	62	3.3350
29	0.1007	46	0.4096	63	4.3294
30	0.1088	47	0.4496	64	5.9925
31	0.1175	48	0.4946	65	9.3272
32	0.1270	49	0.5453	66	19.3486
33	0.1374	50	0.6029		
34	0.1487	51	0.6686		

value quotient). In part B, multiply the answer from part A by the four-digit factor next to your age under column B in Figure 7-1. To demonstrate, let's return to the example of our hypothetical worker who is 31 years old, earns $30,640, and has $12,500 saved.

The next two parts refer to earlier steps already completed. In part C, multiply 0.0995 by the future salary at age 67 that was determined in Step 2. The product will give the dollar amount that must be saved annually. Then divide the product by the worker's current salary in part D. This will give the percentage that must be saved from every paycheck.

We have now completed the fifth and final step. The hypothetical worker in our example needs to save 16.24 percent from each paycheck. Further, for the worker to maintain her standard of living going forward in life, she will most likely want to continue saving this same percentage from the rest of her future paychecks as well. She will hopefully receive many pay raises and bonuses throughout her lifetime. Nonetheless, she will want to keep putting away 16.24 percent of all future pay. Doing so will likely protect her standard of living in retirement. Saving 16.24 percent will probably make her a millionaire by age 67 and independently wealthy. She should never have to worry about running out of money or having her standard of living diminished for as long as she lives.

A Matter of Perspective

You have just completed setting a retirement goal. It is probably a much higher number than you had imagined. It is likely the same story with your savings measurement number. Perhaps you are wondering how you could possibly be that far behind in your savings. And then there is the dollar amount or percentage from each paycheck you should be saving now. These numbers may very well appear way out of reach. If this is the case, don't hit the panic button or give up in despair. Help is on the way in later chapters. It is important now to review these numbers from a broader context or perspective.

First, let us review your goal for retirement. Becoming financially independent is an aggressive goal. Financial independence costs more than your home, more than an Ivy League college degree, and more than all the cars you'll probably ever own in your lifetime. What you are trying to do, after all, is replace your job. That, in essence, is how you determine a valid retirement goal—it is the cost of your job. The value of your job and your retirement goal are the same thing. They both carry the exact price tag. You are wealthy, in other words, if you have enough money to buy your job.

Second to the cost of your job, or goal for retirement, is the cost of a home. Few ever have the resources to pay cash for a home. Most finance these big-ticket purchases. Loans often extend for as long as 30 years. Many families spend as much as 25 to 30 percent of their gross incomes on monthly mortgage payments. The financial obligations associated with home ownership are very well understood by most working Americans. For example, the overwhelming majority of homeowners hope to someday own their residences outright. Home ownership is rightly perceived as a meaningful privilege.

Meanwhile, the average 401(k) deferral among eligible employees in the United States is somewhere around 7 percent of one's gross pay. Seven percent is considered by some to be a liberal number. Many estimate the number to be closer to 5 percent of total pay. Let's assume, for our purposes, the higher number of 7 percent. Few people, nonetheless, would ever dream of spending only 7 percent of their gross income on a mortgage. And yet, when you stop to think about it, your job costs much, much more than your house. Retirement, ironically enough, is about the only expenditure people save and plan for wherein they have no idea of the cost. Whenever one is without a realistic goal and proper measurement, it is easy to erroneously believe that just about any number, whether it is 7 or 5 percent of income, will do just fine. Perhaps that is one reason people are genuinely surprised when they first discover the amount of money they must start saving now if they ever want to retire.

Most workers, as you perhaps just discovered, are generally behind in their retirement savings. Many have been inadvertently snared by the nation's transition to an ownership society. The overwhelming majority did not know, 20 years ago, that they would be the ones primarily responsible for their retirements. Few were ever told just how much they must save over a working lifetime when trying to achieve a retirement nest egg large enough to make them financially independent. The message, in hindsight, was rarely framed properly. In addition, 401(k) retirement plans were often explained in terms of bonus or optional savings programs. They were frequently portrayed as a neat little tax advantaged method to squirrel away some extra money for retirement at the government's expense. Sometimes the emphasis at enrollment meetings was put on how to get money out of the 401(k) program by emphasizing the convenience of loan provisions. Somehow, the real message just failed to get out. Such is the nature of living through major economic transitions. It often takes time for change to become apparent and understood. Truth sometimes emerges slowly.

As a general rule of thumb, it is difficult for most people to replace their jobs by retirement age unless they are saving at least 20 percent of their annual income. Some will definitely need to save more and others less, but not much less. Further, it usually takes average workers a good 30 to 40 years to reach their goal. And investment returns, for those with the patience and temperament to invest wisely, should average around 7.2 percent on an annual basis. Unfortunately, these percentages are seldom emphasized at 401(k) enrollment meetings. All too often participants are led to believe that their returns will be significantly higher and that their savings deferrals can be appreciably lower. Meanwhile, the median 401(k) account balance remains below $20,000, and the average worker gets further and further behind.

Whenever you think about your retirement goal in terms of financial independence, try to think within the context of owning your job outright by age 67. It is very similar in concept to owning your home outright. Conceptualizing retirement from the perspective of owning all the economic benefits of your job is one way to realistically visualize financial independence. You replace your job by making monthly payments to yourself. You control the money and you keep all the earnings and profits from your investments. Saving for retirement takes absolutely nothing away from you. Saving instead transfers money from your paycheck to your retirement wealth account for the single purpose of owning your job outright. That, in a nutshell, is what is meant by all the talk about an ownership society: It is about someday owning your job just as you someday hope to own your home. The vehicle for this job ownership is called your 401(k) plan. That is all there is to it.

Understanding Monthly Retirement Savings Payments

When you finished the fifth and final step to your calculations, you came up with two numbers. One is a dollar amount, and the other is a percentage of your income. For example, in the illustration used in this chapter, the dollar amount equaled $4,975, or $415 a month ($4,975 ÷ 12) and the percentage was 16.34. If you get paid more frequently than monthly, then you will want to divide the annual dollar amount by the number of paychecks you receive each year. A person who receives 24 paychecks in a year divides the dollar amount by 24 to find the amount to save each pay period ($4,975 ÷ 24 = $207 each pay period).

The total money you will have at retirement could vary, depending on whether you decide to save the dollar amount or the percentage amount each year. In the first year, the dollar amount and percentage amounts are identical. Thus, the projected totals accumulated at retirement will also be identical as a result of what was saved in year 1. By the second year, however, you will need to decide whether to follow the dollar amount approach or the savings percentage route.

Let's first explore how the dollar amount approach works. If the worker in our illustration saves $415 a month for the next 36 years and earns an average annual return of 7.2 percent on her investments, she will have $1,000,090 at retirement. (This includes the earnings growth of $12,500 already in savings.) This, incidentally, is her retirement goal. This goal assumes that her wages will increase by 2 percent each year for the next 36 years. A monthly payment made out to her that earns the 7.2 percent on average will basically give her $1 million by age 67. This type of approach could work quite well for the investor as long as her wages do not increase more than 2 percent each year. Interestingly, the dollar approach will eventually become less and less of an annual percentage of her pay, as the dollar savings amount remains fixed while her wages increase over time. There are some professions or jobs wherein the workers can count on a 1 or 2 percent annual increase in wages every year. For these types of occupations, the fixed dollar approach could work. The great risk, however, is inflation. Should one start earning more than a 2 percent increase each year, the dollar approach will likely cause him or her to fall short of the goal. Another risk lies in the expected investment return. Because the return of 7.2 percent is not guaranteed, an extended earnings shortfall could cause one to come up short at retirement as well. Nonetheless, those who are comfortable with the projected earnings and inflation assumptions as outlined in the earlier formulas, can save to replace their jobs in much the same fashion as paying off a home mortgage.

The second course is to base one's savings on a uniform percentage of pay. The illustration outlined in Step 5 indicated that the worker should save 16.34 percent of her pay. This approach is much more conservative than the dollar method. Here the worker simply continues to save 16.34 percent each year. By adopting a saving approach based on a percentage of pay, the worker could even overshoot the goal at retirement. Each year, in other words, the worker will save more money than those on the fixed dollar course, as long as her wages continue to increase. Because she is typically saving more money over time using this method, there is an added measure of protection should inflation spiral upward or investment returns fall short of expectations. As you know, it is nearly impossible to predict what inflation or investments will do over long periods of time. People only get one lifetime to save for retirement, so it is clearly preferable, from my perspective, to get comfortable saving a fairly uniform percentage of one's wages each pay period for as long as one continues to work.

It is a good idea to analyze your retirement situation at least once a year by performing the five steps. Take a few minutes to review your goal, check your progress, and double-check the percentage of pay you need to be saving. Always remember, the road to retirement is not a linear process. It is unlikely that you'll move ahead in nice predictable increments of 7.2 percent each year. Expect instead some years of terrific volatility, and some long, dry stretches that seem to be all work and no progress. That is why it is a good idea to keep saving uniform percentages of pay each year. Good, solid investments, if they lag or fall behind, should eventually come around and catch up with your savings. Saving—and this is so very important—is the controlling key throughout the early process of wealth creation.

FIGURE 7-2 *Retirement Worksheet*

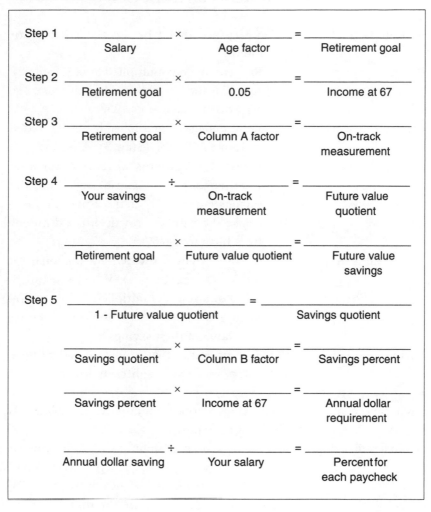

Step 1 _____ × _____ = _____
           Salary   Age factor   Retirement goal

Step 2 _____ × _____ = _____
     Retirement goal   0.05   Income at 67

Step 3 _____ × _____ = _____
     Retirement goal   Column A factor   On-track
                                     measurement

Step 4 _____ ÷ _____ = _____
      Your savings   On-track   Future value
                     measurement   quotient

_____ × _____ = _____
     Retirement goal   Future value quotient   Future value
                                     savings

Step 5 _____ = _____
    1 - Future value quotient   Savings quotient

_____ × _____ = _____
   Savings quotient   Column B factor   Savings percent

_____ × _____ = _____
   Savings percent   Income at 67   Annual dollar
                                  requirement

_____ ÷ _____ = _____
  Annual dollar saving   Your salary   Percent for
                                  each paycheck

Personal Retirement Review

Retirement goal	Salary multiplied by the age-based factor (Step 1).
Income at age 67	Retirement goal multiplied by 0.05 (Step 2). Age 67 is the Social Security retirement age for workers born after 1959.
On-track measurement	Retirement goal multiplied by the age-based Column A factor (Step 3). The on-track measurement helps workers determine whether they are ahead of or behind the savings curve. The on-track measurement tracks the rate of growth on seed money from birth to age 67.
Future value quotient	Current savings divided by the on-track measurement (Step 4). When the future value quotient is multiplied by the retirement goal, workers can determine the future value of their savings.
Savings quotient	The difference that results when the future value quotient is subtracted from part A (Step 5).
Savings percent	Savings quotient multiplied by Column B factor (Step 5).
Annual dollar requirement	Savings percent multiplied by income at age 67. When the savings percent is multiplied by the income at age 67 (Step 2), workers can determine the dollar amount they must save annually (Step 5).
Percent for each paycheck	Annual savings requirement divided by one's current salary (Step 5). This is the percent workers must save from each paycheck.

CHAPTER 8

The Early
Saving Years

Accumulating the first $100,000 from a standing start, with no seed money,
is the most difficult part of building wealth.
Charlie Munger

When my dad was 26 years old, he was in England. One day in June he and a group of friends were called together for an important briefing. He was in the Army. The commanding officer informed the group that within the next few days they would be departing for France. The officer then made a peculiar request. "Men," he barked, "I want you to turn your heads to the right and take a good, long look at your buddy." The officer continued, "The casualty rate for our unit will be 50 percent. That means either you or the guy next to you won't make it when we land on Omaha Beach." Upon hearing the horrible news of a probable death sentence, the entire outfit immediately burst into laughter. My dad said even he started laughing as well. None could imagine getting killed. Everyone thought the other guy would get hit.

One of the hardest things for 20- and 30-year-olds to do is actually believe they will either get old or die. That is just the way our brains operate. While Warren Buffett laments the fact that investors are prone to look out the rearview mirror instead of through the windshield, he is careful not to say looking through the windshield is easy. For some inexplicable reason, embracing the future or the unforeseen is extremely counterintuitive. We seem to have an innate tendency to gravitate toward the familiar and seen, even when we know better from a rational perspective.

Twenty- and 30-year-olds have a tremendous advantage with regard to wealth creation. It is time. Time generally benefits all things that grow. Time—like air, water, fire, and food—is a commodity that one never wants to exhaust. Those with an abundance of time are almost assured of becoming wealthy, provided they start saving now and remain on that path. That is why it is so good to be a 20- or 30-year-old. Wealth favors the young. To be even more specific, if you are in your 20s or your early 30s, you can become financially independent, provided you work at it. There is still enough time.

As we review those who are somewhere between 20 and 39 years of age, it might be helpful to explore in detail a second hypothetical worker who is 30 years old. Age 30 splits the difference between these two decades evenly. The hypothetical worker profiled for our study has a decent job that pays $37,200. Like many in her age group, however, she has put nothing away for retirement. This person, nonetheless, wants very much to retire wealthy. The worker is clear in her understanding that she must look to the future and give up the rearview mirror forever.

The second hypothetical 30-year-old worker earning $37,200 will have a retirement goal at age 67 of $1,238,388 (see Figure 5-1, Chapter 5). To achieve this goal, the worker will need to save $562 each month, or about 18 percent of her annual pay (see Figure 6-1, Chapter 6, and Figure 7-1, Chapter 7). She has 37 years to become a millionaire. There is plenty of time to accomplish her goal, provided she remains committed to the savings program.

Saving 18 percent from each paycheck may likely cause our hypothetical worker to establish a monthly income statement to closely monitor her expenses. Expenses can easily soak up every single cent a person earns. Focusing on future wealth gives investors a strong incentive to wring money out of their monthly earnings and invest those savings before expenses soak it all up. It is largely a matter of individual priorities. Workers who want to retire wealthy must make it their top priority to build their monthly budget around savings requirements and goals. Whenever future retirement wealth is the fourth, fifth, sixth, or seventh monthly budget priority, deferred savings will generally prove insufficient to support a goal in excess of $1 million by retirement age. Expenses, as a general rule, revolve around the axis of personal priorities. Priorities, in a word, determine ultimately how and where money gets spent. To retire wealthy, workers must make it their number one priority to save for retirement.

Monthly Income Statement for the 30-Year-Old Worker

Monthly income	$3,100	
Retirement savings		560
Rent		870
Utilities		200
Groceries		400
Taxes		500
Charity		20
Transportation		200
Medical		30
Entertainment		120
Vacations		200
Total Expenses		$3,100

One of the most significant results of a family budget or personal income statement is the actual listing of spending priorities. As a practical matter, it is extremely difficult to control how every last cent gets spent in a family budget. Families do not operate like businesses. The typical family will get bushwhacked by more financial surprises in a week than a business generally does in a full year. A family budget can, however, set priorities. The first dollars earned can get saved for retirement. The next dollars pay the necessary operating costs such as rent, utilities, groceries, and taxes. The rest, then, largely gets juggled. The operative word when balancing the family checkbook is *flexibility*. Honor the major priorities, and then just let the dust clear. That is usually the way it works in a normal household. Chaos management supplants financial theory. It is a happy fact of life.

In the illustration with our hypothetical worker, she must save 18 percent of her income in order to retire wealthy. Few—very few—people will ever achieve financial independence by saving substantially less than 20 percent of their gross incomes. Annually, she will want to refigure the calculations or measurements, because the road to retirement is fluid. Circumstances change. Investors must make it a habit to continually monitor their progress at least once a year to prevent unpleasant surprises at retirement.

The Most Difficult Part of Building Wealth

Charlie Munger is on record as saying, "Accumulating the first $100,000 from a standing start, with no seed money, is the most difficult part of building wealth."[1] Why? Because mastering the most difficult part to any process is often the key to success. Although Munger does not say it, one can nonetheless infer by his observation that whenever a person figures out how to accumulate $100,000, that individual worker stands an excellent chance of being able find his or her way home. That is why it is so important to understand how one gets from zero net worth to $100,000 in savings in a timely fashion.

It might be helpful to return to our hypothetical worker to develop a clear picture of how one accumulates the first $100,000. The worker in our most recent example is 30 years old and earns $37,200 annually. Her retirement goal at age 67 is $1,238,388. She has elected to save $562 of her monthly income for the next 37 years to reach her goal. Assuming she invests in a mutual fund with a 7.2 percent annual average rate of return, it will take this investor 122 months, or 10 years and 2 months, to reach $100,000. Over this decade of saving and investing, the worker contributes a total of $68,564. The stock market or mutual fund contributes $31,436 in earnings. The $100,000 is therefore comprised of three very important factors: time, 122 months; savings, $68,564; and earnings, $31,436.

As this breakdown indicates, the worker has to put in almost 70 cents on every dollar, which eventually accumulates to $100,000. When we round the numbers, the worker saves $70,000, and the market earns $30,000. The worker, as you can see clearly, is doing most all the heavy lifting. Without saving significant sums, it is very unlikely she could ever accumulate $100,000 within 10 years. One reason, then, that accumulating the first $100,000 is so difficult, is that the investor has to do almost all the work. When reaching toward that first $100,000, the market does not help all that much. Individual savings is the engine pulling the train.

Many workers and investors underestimate the significance of savings, especially in the early years of wealth creation. The emphasis, instead, is often on investments and investment returns. Participants in 401(k) plans are often educated on stocks and bonds, large cap and small cap, high beta and low beta, and alpha, and the importance of international funds. The tenor of these retirement meetings generally favors the importance of learning how to invest. Learning about investing and investments is certainly worthwhile and positive. There is, however, a "time for every season." When in the early years of personal wealth creation, it is a time for saving.

To illustrate the point further, let's conduct a couple of experiments. The first experiment will involve three investors. Net worth for each is zero. The three are in a race to reach $10,000. Each investor will save $500 a month. The first investor will invest in a mutual fund and receive a 7.2 percent average annual rate of return. The second investor is a real financial wizard. She will work her magic to achieve a 10.8 percent average annual return. Her investments will outperform the first investor's by 50 percent. Many professionals on Wall Street would kill to get her results. The third investor is ultraconservative. She has put all her money in a sock hidden under the mattress. The starting gun fires, and the race begins! The hotshot investor obviously gets to $10,000 first. It takes her 19 months. The investor who purchased the mutual fund earning an average return of 7.2 percent arrived at $10,000 in second place. It, incredibly enough, was a close second. She was only hours behind the hotshot investor whose investment performance was 50 percent better. It also took her 19 months to reach $10,000. Finally, there is the timid investor who hid her money under the mattress. She was only a few days behind. It took her 20 months to reach the goal of $10,000. The point is exceedingly apparent. Personal savings, in the early years, is the dominant determinant with regard to wealth creation. The effect of stellar investment returns, as seen in this example, is usually negligible.

Let's look at one more experiment before proceeding further. Two investors want to race all the way to $100,000, which is the most difficult part of becoming wealthy. The first investor will save $500 a month and get a fabulous investment return of 10.8 percent. The second investor will invest in a mutual fund and receive an average annual return of 7.2 percent. The first investor will have a 50 percent advantage over the second investor in terms of investment returns. The second investor, hoping to compensate for the smaller return, puts in more hours at work by working overtime. She takes the extra money and applies it to her savings. She will save $750 a month, instead of $500 a month, for a 50 percent advantage in savings. So, we have two very competitive contestants. One will save 50 percent more than her competitor. The other will earn 50 percent more on her investments. The starting gun fires, and the race begins. The first investor reaches $100,000 in 115 months, or 9 years and 7 months. The investor who worked overtime and saved extra money reached $100,000 in 98 months, or 8 years and 2 months. The race was not even close. Again, as demonstrated in this second experiment, saving is the engine that pulls the train in the early years.

Think back to the earlier stories of Warren Buffett. When Buffett was building his seed money, he did very little investing. He bought his first stock at age 11 and then shifted wealth strategies. Buffett started peddling papers, selling golf balls, and leasing used pinball machines. Instead of putting his hard-earned money in the market, Buffett stuffed dollars away in his bedroom chest-of-drawers. He seemed to understand at a remarkably early age that saving and under spending was the first step to wealth creation. Those who concentrate on investing in the early years, at the expense of saving and under spending, are likely to miss the train altogether.

The most difficult part of building wealth is accumulating the first $100,000 because the investor must do just about all the work. Buffett delivered 600,000 newspapers, Munger practiced law and drove an old, yellow clunker with a secondhand paint job, and Benjamin Franklin had a reputation for getting up early and opening his shop ahead of all the other merchants in Philadelphia. Each man, in his own way, was becoming wealthy. They were single-handedly putting together seed money by working long, hard hours. Likewise, the investor in our sample illustration beat the investment wiz in the race to $100,000 by working overtime for eight years. The effort required to achieve the first $100,000 is a story seldom told in 401(k) enrollment meetings. Munger's observations on reaching the first $100,000 are not rhetorical. Achieving the first $100,000 is difficult. You have to work hard at your job, under spend your income, and make saving your top financial priority. These are words you can take to the bank.

The Impact of Investing

Saving is the first critical component to the process of wealth creation. When accumulating wealth, a person must always save. Further, when in the early years, the extent to which one saves could very likely determine whether one is able to ever achieve financial independence.

But, as one might imagine, saving, although exceedingly important, is not the whole story. Investing and investment returns also play a vital role in the creation and accumulation of wealth.

The importance of investing and investment returns becomes significant once a person has accumulated the first $100,000: $100,000, in this regard, serves as an important milestone wherein investing begins to emerge as the dominant determinant in personal wealth creation. While saving carries the freight from zero net worth to the first $100,000, investing and investment returns will shoulder the burden of getting the worker from $100,000 to $1 million. Once an investor reaches $100,000 in retirement net worth, it is time for investing.

Let's return to the hypothetical worker with the retirement goal of $1,238,388. When she achieved the first $100,000, we learned that approximately 70 percent of the money came from personal savings, while the balance of $30,000 resulted from a 7.2 percent investment return. Starting from a base of zero, it took her 122 months (10 years and 2 months) to reach $100,000. There are now 26 years and 10 months (322 months) remaining for her to accumulate $1,138,388, which is the balance of her retirement goal. Our hypothetical worker will continue to save $562 a month, and her mutual fund will continue to deliver a 7.2 percent average annual return. Sure enough, 26 years and 10 months later, our investor reaches her goal of $1,238,338. Surprisingly, the mutual fund delivered 84 percent of the balance ($957,424), while personal savings only contributed 16 percent, or $180,964. Once she hit the first $100,000, earnings from the mutual fund took over. For every $1 the investor saved, the mutual fund pumped in more than $5 from earnings. The roles of saving and investing reversed after the investor reached the first $100,000.

There are at least two critically important themes investors must understand when accumulating $100,000. First, investors must realize that they will be doing nearly all the work. Investment returns do not really start to "kick in" until the $100,000 mark has been achieved. Second, there is not much time to get the job done. The longer it takes a person to reach $100,000, the less likely it is that one will retire wealthy. If I could only make one statement at a 401(k) enrollment meeting, it would be this: Get to $100,000 as quickly as possible by saving as much as possible.

For the worker with zero net worth or hardly anything put away in savings, it is often very difficult to envision ever achieving $1 million in savings or one's prescribed retirement goal. There is good news, however, for the doubting or skeptical worker. There is help waiting at the $100,000 mark. At $100,000, the emphasis shifts away from the narrow focus on saving and broadens out to include investing and investment returns. Saving is still critical, but there are other contributing factors that will benefit the worker at $100,000. The burden, hence, gets lighter. The road becomes easier to travel. Your feet are lighter, and you begin to travel faster as the pace accelerates at this important milestone.

Setting Priorities

There is an old expression that has nearly become cliché: *Pay yourself first.* Nonetheless, this tired phrase still makes a lot of sense. Inherent in this phrase is a subtle admonition to approach the future with caution. Look out for number one. Watch your wallet. The demands on your paycheck are countless. Make sure, in other words, that present necessities and desires do not overwhelm your ability to provide for future needs. *Pay yourself first* so that you do not stray and get yourself into financial trouble. It is an excellent motto by which to firmly establish spending priorities. Nothing gets spent until retirement savings have been met. The hypothetical worker's monthly income statement noted earlier in this chapter highlights this motif perfectly. The very first monthly budget item is labeled retirement savings. It typically requires this exact kind of focus to retire wealthy.

Such a pronounced focus on saving for retirement will undoubtedly raise many interesting questions. For instance, a younger worker might legitimately ask about the merits of purchasing a house. Is not a home, after all, a worthy investment? Further, could not one also argue favorably that a home is an investment in the future? How does home ownership, in other words, weigh against retirement savings for the younger worker? Should young workers save simultaneously for both a down payment and retirement goals? Home ownership, for instance, has traditionally been a terrific investment for most American families.

Home ownership is no doubt essential to an ownership society. It serves most workers well to own their homes. Ownership, as discussed earlier, brings stability to families. Workers should make serious provisions to own their homes outright by retirement age. Home ownership,

however, does have several limitations with regard to personal wealth creation. Namely, houses do not produce income, unless one is investing in
rental properties. The purpose of retirement savings is to accumulate assets that can be converted into income-producing investments by retirement age. Houses generally appreciate in value based on increases in
inflation and regional population growth. Houses, in this regard, can
sometimes turn out to be excellent investments, but homes are difficult
to convert into income-producing vehicles at retirement, unless one
chooses to rent out the upstairs rooms or to sell out altogether, pocket a
gain, and move into a less expensive residence.

Once one gets established in a job or career, there is nonetheless a
pronounced interest on the part of most workers to save for a down
payment and purchase a home. The rationalization often follows the
lines that paying rent is analogous to throwing money away. Why pay
rent when one could be building equity in a home? It is a common question among younger workers who are getting some financial traction in
their lives.

When we purchased our first home, I was 38 years old. It took, after
graduating from high school, 20 years to buy a home. The house was a
two-bedroom starter home. My wife, who was also very committed to
saving and investing, was nonetheless anxious to settle down and establish "roots." Just prior to our home purchase, we were living in a garden
home, which is a fancy word for a duplex. It was our belief, a belief, incidentally, that has only strengthened over the years, that one should
first accumulate $100,000 in retirement savings before purchasing a
home. The logic is simple. The most difficult part of becoming wealthy
is accumulating the first $100,000. Nothing, absolutely no single discre-
tionary expenditure of any meaningful substance, save a college degree, should ever precede the most difficult hurdle to becoming
wealthy. Get to $100,000 in savings and then shop for a house. Interest-
ingly, the guy who lived in the other half of our garden home was a professional football player for the Chicago Bears. He could have owned
almost any house in town. Instead he and his wife were sharing a roof
and common wall with the Roses. He was living way below his means
and saving diligently so that he would be financially secure upon retiring from the NFL.

Warren Buffett seems to have followed a similar strategy. His net
worth had easily surpassed $100,000 before he purchased his first home.

He, too, had several kids before ever buying a home. Buffett still lives in that same house. It is on a fairly busy street in Omaha. Buffett's taste in residential property is perhaps an undisguised commentary on how the second richest man in America views the investment merits of home ownership.

Another matter of considerable concern for workers surrounds the whole matter of children. Kids, in short, are expensive. Furthermore, children grow even more expensive as they age. There is nothing economical about rearing children. Kids can become real fiscal "budget busters" if not managed properly.

The old, worn saying of *pay yourself first* applies additionally to all the expenses related to children. Saving for retirement, if one is to retire financially independent and not become a burden, must retain primacy over all financial commitments, including children. Budgets are not elastic. Household finances have real limits. Expenses, even when tied to heartstrings, are secondary to retirement needs when one adopts the mandate to get paid first.

Those who *pay themselves first* soon learn there are many things in life they simply cannot afford. One such expense for many working Americans is the cost of providing a college education for their children. There are literally millions and millions of household budgets that are simply incapable of stretching monthly paychecks to include retirement savings, home ownership, and the cost of college for kids. It is an economic reality.

Surprisingly, the consequence of not being able to afford college tuition for youngsters is not altogether negative. While perhaps not readily apparent, students who pay their way through college often gain a tremendous advantage in life. Underscoring this, the authors to the *Millionaire Next Door,* Charles Stanley and William Danko, discovered that nearly half of the millionaires they studied "never received any college tuition from their parents or other relatives."[2] Paying one's way through college, in other words, is not a bad prerequisite for becoming a millionaire.

Children who have to figure out a way to foot the bill for college often pick up an additional degree of self-sufficiency. They master, in addition to their college studies, the science of ingenuity, independence, and industry; qualities that handily facilitate the building of personal wealth over time later in life. Those who pay their way through college are in many respects blessed. It can be a tremendous gift to bestow upon a child.

The road to retirement, in the final analysis, basically boils down to individual priorities. Those who overspend for houses and take on additional financial responsibilities beyond their budgets are likely to fall way behind in retirement savings. Although a bit tired, worn, and overused, the cliché to *pay yourself first* is anything but glib. Those who pay themselves first are inevitably forced to confront numerous financial decisions that are difficult and tough. There is nothing easy about saying no to expenditures that tug at the heartstrings. Yet, few ever achieve $100,000 in net worth on a timely basis without saying no over and over and over again. That is one reason it is so difficult to achieve the first step of $100,000. Such a vital financial accomplishment demands a worker to be resolute, hard-nosed, and determined. Wealth creation, as we have observed, is largely a self-controlled process grounded in personal saving priorities.

CHAPTER 9

Catching Up on Retirement Savings in Your 40s and 50s

We never see the true state of our condition, till it is illustrated to us by its contraries.
Robinson Crusoe

Financial Security in Retirement

The question for many workers in their 40s and 50s who are saving and investing earnestly for retirement is this: How do I catch up? They have calculated their retirement goal, measured their savings progress, and reviewed their deferral amounts. Now that the savings assessment process is completed, they are honestly perplexed. A million dollars by retirement age appears mathematically impossible.

As noted in earlier chapters, it became clear that one could never grasp Charlie Munger without reading Benjamin Franklin and Daniel Defoe. While it was a treat to revisit Franklin, I was in no hurry to go back and study *Robinson Crusoe,* a subject that should have been mastered by high school graduation. Surprisingly, and this was a genuine surprise, the story of *Crusoe* was immensely helpful. It, in many ways, is the perfect corollary for those in their 40s and 50s who must figure out how to become financially secure with only half the time available to 20- and 30-year-olds. The story of *Robinson Crusoe* gives the middle-aged reader who wishes to retire a critical starting point for answering the ubiquitous question, What must one do to catch up?

The model adopted by Crusoe applies to almost anyone regardless of his or her present station or ultimate goal in life. Once one can determine where it is he or she wishes to end up in life (for instance, becoming financially independent by retirement age) one must first take inventory of available resources. Lifetime destinies, in other words, begin with a goal, and then progress forward from personal resources readily obtainable. Shipwrecked, abandoned, disoriented, and perilously close to complete exhaustion, Crusoe's situation was as close to hopeless as one can get in life. Before throwing in the towel and surrendering to fate, however, Crusoe somehow discovered the presence of mind to take inventory of his resources. It was a stroke of brilliance. It, in fact, saved his life by giving him what he most needed at this desperately low point in his story. Once Crusoe finished taking inventory of all the resources available to him, he found hope. Crusoe reasoned, after adding up all the positives and then weighing them against the negatives, that he would prevail. There was not a single negative on his list that could defeat him.

The negatives for middle-aged workers who wish to retire are very well known. First, there is a serious lack of time. It takes, as discussed earlier, 30 to 40 years of saving and investing to become wealthy, but many in their 40s and 50s have very little put away for retirement. Much time, in other words, has passed without the effect of building financial assets. This unproductive passage of time is a very real negative, affecting literally millions. Then there are the tremendous financial demands of raising a family; all know the unending expenses of groceries and clothing, as well as insurance, medical, and monthly utility bills. Additionally, there are often debts such as credit cards, mortgages, car loans, outstanding balances at department stores, and various other types of consumer obligations. Just as Crusoe was vividly aware of all the negatives threatening his life when he found himself washed up on a strange shore, today's workers are no less encumbered by real obligations that legitimately threaten their financial livelihoods. It requires little imagination to extend the column listing negatives when examining all the factors that could prevent one from retiring financially independent.

The structure of life is such that those who pursue difficult goals will almost always confront tremendous obstacles or genuine negatives. Obstacles, in other words, are a given. Those who achieve difficult goals figure out how to overcome obstacles. Countering negatives with positives, or overcoming obstacles with resources, is the lesson Robinson Crusoe had to quickly master on the island. To survive, Crusoe had to first design a blueprint for success. This is one reason the story of *Robinson Crusoe* is such an enduring masterpiece. Defoe's *Crusoe* is a captivating adventure that subtly uncovers simple keys to success any reader can apply to his or her own life.

When applying Robinson Crusoe's formulas for success to present-day circumstances of insufficient retirement savings, it is helpful to note one of Crusoe's very first acts on the island. Prior to listing his two columns—one column naming obstacles and the other identifying resources—Crusoe redefined his ultimate goal. His initial hope was to get off the island for good and return home to England. Such a spectacular dream, however, was completely out of the question. Crusoe just simply lacked the resources. He instead redirected his efforts toward the more reasonable goals of surviving and acclimating himself to his newly discovered home. Because he could not get back to England, Crusoe decided on the second-best objective available to him: to prevail over the elements of a foreign wilderness and live life as fully as possible.

It will be exceedingly difficult for middle-aged 50-year-olds who are seriously behind in their retirement savings to achieve financial independence within 17 or 20 years when it typically takes the average worker anywhere from 30 to 40 years. Like Crusoe, many middle-aged workers will need to redefine their ultimate goal. The retirement goal of financial independence must be changed to a more practical objective of financial security. *Financial security* can be understood as combining one's personal money with outside resources to maintain that individual's standard of living in retirement. Financial security differs from financial independence in that those who are financially secure depend, in some measure, on these outside resources. An example of an outside resource, for instance, is Social Security. Financially secure persons in retirement, who lack the financial assets to be completely financially independent, are able to maintain their basic lifestyles by coupling personal retirement assets with those provided by the government. The planning strategy of financial security works exceedingly well for older and middle-aged workers, as long as the government does not adversely change the rules or drastically reduce anticipated benefits. This is the one major caveat to financial security as opposed to financial independence: Dependency on outside resources means entities other than the individual worker, usually the government, *own and control* these outside assets. Nevertheless, once the retirement goal of financial independence is changed to financial security, workers now count future Social Security benefits as an additional resource available to them in retirement.

Whenever there is a shortage of time and insufficient savings but an abundance of household expenses or obligations, one must consider altering the retirement goal from financial independence to financial security. Once done, there are generally several resources available to workers. First, there is Social Security. Second, there is the time remaining until one's retirement. Time, as we shall soon discover, is a very important resource whenever one decides to work just a few years beyond normal retirement age. And finally, many workers will have access to vested interests in either pension assets or monthly pension income. Amazingly, these varied resources often signify hundreds of thousands of dollars.

The significance of retirement savings is sometimes never fully appreciated until one approaches the eve of retirement with insufficient sums. "We never see the true state of our condition," wrote Daniel Defoe in 1719, "till it is illustrated to us by its contraries."[1] Once obstacles, even very great obstacles, are recognized, however, people will often bear down and figure out a way to prevail when the will and resources are present. That, in short, is one key aspect to the inspiring message of *Robinson Crusoe:* Individual will coupled with resources pull people forward toward the completion of successful endeavors.

Calculating the Impact of Social Security and Savings

The contribution Social Security makes to most workers who are seeking personal financial security in retirement is exceedingly significant. To explore the positive impact of Social Security in greater detail, we will create a hypothetical worker who is 50 years of age. First, the worker's retirement goal will be determined in light of her age, salary, and savings. Then we will measure her savings progress and define what she must begin saving now to retire independently wealthy. We will next take this same worker and assess her retirement circumstances by adding monthly Social Security payments to her future income. These studies will require some arithmetic calculations based on one new table and the charts already covered in earlier chapters.

Hypothetical Worker

Age	50
Salary	$45,000
Savings	$25,000

The worker's retirement goal is easily calculated by multiplying the $45,000 salary times the age factor of 22.40 in Figure 5-1 (Step 1). Accordingly, the retirement goal at age 67 for our hypothetical worker is $1,008,000. Her annual income at age 67 will need to equal $50,400 ($1,008,000 × 0.05) (Step 2). When we measure her savings progress, by multiplying the retirement goal times the Column A factor in Figure 6-1 (Step 3), it is discovered that she is far behind ($309,153 vs. $25,000). Based on this information, we can define what she must start saving now to retire independently wealthy using Figure 7-1 (Step 5), which is $2,328 a month, or 62 percent of her current income of $45,000! Obviously, few workers earning $45,000 have the means to save $27,930 annually. It is apparent that financial independence is out of the question for this particular 50-year-old worker. Too much time has passed with too little saving.

Our attention shall now focus on securing financial security in retirement for this worker by utilizing her Social Security benefits. Each year, workers eligible to receive Social Security benefits typically receive in the mail a statement of projected monthly benefits at retirement age. These statements show three potential retirement ages: 62, 65, 66, or 67, depending on one's date of birth; and 70. Our calculations here will use 67 as the normal retirement age. The later one begins receiving benefits, the higher the monthly payments. Because the worker in this illustration is hypothetical, we shall estimate her Social Security benefits. When you, however, perform your individual calculations, make sure to use those projected benefits provided by the Social Security Administration. The calculations in our examples will accommodate those numbers provided for you by Social Security.

Social Security benefits are projected as monthly payments, so it will be necessary to convert the goal at retirement, as well as the future value of one's savings, into monthly income. After these conversions have been made, the sum of all these monthly payments will be tallied into a final worksheet. Once the final worksheet is complete, workers will learn what they must start saving now to reach financial security by retirement age.

Step 1: Monthly Retirement Income Goal

As we already noted, the retirement goal for our hypothetical worker was determined by multiplying her annual income of $45,000 by the age factor (22.40) found in Figure 5-1. This produced a retirement goal of $1,008,000. The monthly income goal is found by multiplying her retirement goal by 0.00417.[2] The hypothetical worker in our illustration will therefore need $4,200 each month in retirement ($1,008,000 × 0.00417 = $4,200) (rounded).

Step 2: Retirement Monthly Income from Current Savings

We shall employ a new calculation to determine the future value of our hypothetical worker's $25,000 in retirement savings. Figure 9-1 lists factors that determine the future value of money.[3] The worker in our example is 50 years old and wants to retire by age 67. This means she has 17 years until her retirement (Age 67 – Age 50 = 17 years). Next to 17, under the Years column in Figure 9-1, is the factor 3.261. To find the future value 17 years from now of $25,000, multiply $25,000 by 3.261. The answer is $81,525. This represents the growth of $25,000 over 17 years at an annual compounded rate of return of 7.2 percent.

Next we will want to figure out what $81,525 will produce in monthly income. Here, we will multiply $81,525 by 0.00417. The answer is $340 (rounded). The monthly income produced by $81,525 is $340.

When adding current retirement savings, make sure you include all the money in your 401(k), Individual Retirement Accounts (IRAs), additional money in IRA rollover accounts, and any money that might be with a former employer, as well as any other savings that are clearly designated for retirement. The sum of all these accounts will equal your current retirement savings.

Step 3: Monthly Income from Social Security

This step is unbelievably easy. All you have to do is take the projected monthly payment provided to you by the Social Security Administration.

FIGURE 9-1 *Future Value Asset Chart*

Years	Factor	Years	Factor	Years	Factor
1	1.072	15	2.837	28	7.006
2	1.149	16	3.042	29	7.510
3	1.232	17	3.261	30	8.051
4	1.321	18	3.495	31	8.631
5	1.416	19	3.747	32	9.252
6	1.518	20	4.017	33	9.918
7	1.627	21	4.306	34	10.63
8	1.744	22	4.616	35	11.39
9	1.870	23	4.949	36	12.22
10	2.002	24	5.305	37	13.09
11	2.149	25	5.687	38	14.04
12	2.303	26	6.096	39	15.05
13	2.469	27	6.535	40	16.13
14	2.647				

Because this is a hypothetical illustration, we shall estimate that our worker will receive $1,944 a month upon retiring at age 67.

Step 4: Required Monthly Savings to Reach Financial Security in Retirement

As we can see from the preceding review, monthly Social Security checks and income from savings alone will not satisfy our hypothetical worker's monthly income requirements, based upon her retirement goal for age 67. She must therefore continue to save and invest from each paycheck. To calculate exactly what our worker must save, we should first add her Social Security payments and her future saving monthly payments: $1,944 + $340 = $2,284. We now need to subtract the monthly income of $2,284 from her monthly income goal of $4,200. The result is $1,916. This is the monthly amount our hypothetical worker must figure out a way to generate by age 67.

To calculate what this worker must save each month, we need to multiply $1,916 by the factor under Column B in Figure 7-1 (0.6029 × $1,916). The answer is $1,155. This is the amount she must save each month for the next 17 years to achieve financial security in retirement.

FIGURE 9-2 *Calculating the Impact of Social Security and Savings*

Age	50
Retirement age	67
Salary	$45,000
Savings	$25,000
Step 1	
Goal	$1,008,000
Monthly retirement target	$4,200
Step 2	
Future income from savings	$340
Step 3	
Social Security	<u>$1,944</u>
	$2,284
Step 4	
Amount needed to save monthly	$4,200
	<u>$2,284</u>
	$1,916
Column B (0.6029) × $1916 =	$1,155
Amount needed to save monthly	$1,155

Unfortunately, however, $1,155 is a rather significant percent of the worker's monthly paycheck. It represents approximately 31 percent of her current pay (defined as gross pay, before taxes are taken out). As a practical matter, it generally is difficult to save more than 20 percent of one's pretax paycheck. It is likely that this particular worker will want to achieve financial security by saving a sum each month closer to 20 percent of her income, or near $750 dollars a month. In the spirit of Robinson Crusoe, we must now turn to yet another resource. We shall next explore the economic impact of extending one's working career by just three years.

Calculating the Significance of Three Years

The velocity of time is much different for a 50-year-old than for a 22-year-old. As strange as it sounds, the older a person gets, the faster time passes through one's senses. A full 365 days means one thing to a

22-year-old and something completely different to someone who is 92 years old. Time quantified by the clock is universal and precise, whereas time measured from an individual perspective is hardly uniform at all. Seniors and young people understand and describe time in much different terms.

Our purpose in this section is to value time from an economic perspective. What is the price tag of time, defined in terms of dollars and cents, for a 50-year-old who is saving diligently in hopes of achieving financial security in retirement? Does it make sense to keep working and postpone retirement until age 70? To address these issues fully, one must first substantiate projections with real numbers that will satisfy economic realities.

Step 1: Monthly Retirement Income Goal

A minor adjustment in her retirement goal needs to be made when extending the retirement age by 3 years for our 50-year old worker. Instead of multiplying her salary by the factor in Figure 5-1 next to age 50, we must instead take the factor next to age 47. This will extend the years left until retirement from 17 to 20 years. Thus, $45,000 times the age 47 factor (23.78) produces a new retirement goal of $1,070,100. Delaying retirement by 3 years in this example increases the goal by $62,100 over the previous goal of $1,008,000 at age 50. This increase is due to the impact of inflation. Each year one delays retiring, it takes more money to compensate for inflation. Time, as defined by working 3 additional years, must therefore more than recompense the worker's investments and savings to stay ahead of inflation, otherwise the additional effort will be compromised.

Once the new retirement goal of $1,070,100 has been established, the remaining arithmetic is very familiar. To determine her monthly income at age 70, we simply multiply $1,070,100 by 0.00417. The result is $4,462 (rounded.) Our 50-year-old worker will need to achieve a monthly income target of $4,462 at age 70.

Step 2: Retirement Monthly Income from Current Savings

Figure 9-1 lists factors that determine the future value of money. The 50-year-old worker in our example now wishes to retire at age 70. This means she has 20 years until retirement (Age 70 – Age 50 = 20 years). Next to 20, under the Years column in Figure 9-1, is the factor 4.017. To find the future value of $25,000 in 20 years, multiply $25,000 by the factor 4.017 ($25,000 × 4.017 = $100,425). The answer, as you can see, is $100,425.

Next we will want to figure out what that $100,425 will produce in monthly income. Again, we simply multiply $100,425 by 0.00417, which produces an answer of $418 (rounded). This represents the annual income generated by an investment of $100,425.

Step 3: Figuring Monthly Social Security Payments at Age 70

Again, this step is unbelievably easy. All you have to do is take your annual statement from the Social Security Administration and find the monthly payment next to your name under monthly retirement income at age 70. For our purposes, we will estimate that our hypothetical worker will receive $2,400 at age 70.

Step 4: Required Monthly Savings to Reach Financial Security in Retirement

Once more, it is necessary to add the Social Security payments with the monthly projected investment income (see Step 3) ($2,400 + $418 = $2,818). The monthly goal is $4,462, so our hypothetical worker will need to make up a difference of $1,644. As you may recall, subtracting the Social Security income and investment income ($2,818) from her monthly retirement income goal ($4,462) produces the difference of $1,644 ($4,462 – $2,818 = $1,644). This is the amount of money our worker needs to figure out how to replace each month at age 70.

To calculate what she must begin saving now to achieve financial security by age 70, our worker needs to take $1,652 and multiply it by the factor next to age 47 under Column B on Figure 7-1, which is 0.4496 (0.4496 × $1644 = $739). Therefore, to retire financially secure at age 70, our worker will need to begin saving $739 (rounded) a month for the next 20 years. This represents approximately 20 percent of her gross monthly income. From a monthly savings viewpoint, her retirement goal is finally within reach. Saving 20 percent over the next 20 years will get the job done.

The Future Value of Monthly Savings

By saving $739 a month, assuming her investments earn an average annual return of 7.2 percent, our hypothetical worker will amass nearly $500,000. Here's how the arithmetic works. First, as we just reviewed, her $25,000 in savings should grow to around $100,000 (see Step 2). Finding the future value of her monthly $739 is also fairly simple to calculate. All we have to do is divide the monthly income our worker is saving to replace by age 70–$1,644–by the monthly income goal of $4,462 ($1,644 ÷ $4,462 = 37 percent).

FIGURE 9-3 *Calculating the Significance of Three Years*

Age	50
Retirement age	70
Salary	$45,000
Savings	$25,000
Step 1	
Goal	$1,070,100
Monthly retirement target	$4,462
Step 2	
Future income from savings	418
Step 3	
Social Security	$2,400
	$2,818
Step 4	
Amount needed to catch up	$1,644
Column B (0.4496) × $1,644 =	$739 (rounded)
Amount needed to save monthly	$739

Now multiply 37 percent by her actual retirement goal at age 70 of $1,072,800, and you will come up with the future value of our worker's monthly savings ($1,070,100 × 0.37 = $395,937). Add $395,937 to $100,000 (the future value of her $25,000 in savings), and you'll get $495,937. This is what our worker should be worth at age 70. Saving $739 a month for 20 years, when added to the future growth of her $25,000 in current savings, will increase her net worth in retirement to nearly a half million dollars. Although this worker is very much behind in her retirement savings, she can basically correct her course by starting now, saving sufficient sums, and working to age 70!

Calculating Pensions and Other Income Sources

For many people, there are additional sources of income that will be available to them in retirement. Some studies suggest that more than half the working population will be entitled to some kind of pension benefit in retirement. Also, some workers have made investments in real estate that produce monthly income. Still others are likely to enhance financial assets in retirement by moving into either less expensive homes or perhaps relocating to lower-cost regions of the country. Many people have made credible provisions for retirement that lie beyond the realm of saving and investing in 401(k) plans or IRAs.

A key question for many workers, however, concerns whether they still need to save additional sums for retirement. The calculations in this chapter can hopefully provide these individuals with additional insight. Future pension income, for example, is treated exactly as future Social Security income in our calculations. All one has to do to determine the need for further saving, is simply combine all the sources of known monthly income together and then subtract from the monthly income goal that was calculated in Step 1.

To illustrate, let us return to our hypothetical worker. She earns $45,000 annually, has $25,000 in savings, and is 50 years of age. She wants to retire financially secure at age 67. In Step 1 we learned that she would need $1,008,000 at age 67. This $1,008,000 will produce $4,200 in monthly income to maintain her standard of living in retirement.

Our hypothetical worker thus begins the process, much in the spirit of Robinson Crusoe, by adding together her resources. According to her Social

Security statement, she is projected to receive a monthly benefit of $1,944 at age 67. Additionally, a former employer still carries a pension in which our worker is fully vested. The pension is projected to pay her $200 a month in retirement. She also inherited a rental property from her father that pays $600 a month. Finally, the future income from her current $25,000 in savings is projected to produce $340 in monthly compensation.

The sum of Social Security, a monthly pension, rental income, and savings will come to $3,084 a month in retirement ($1,944 + $200 + $600 + $340 = $3,084). Subtracting the projected income of $3,084 from her future income goal of $4,200 leaves a difference of $1,116 ($4,200 − $3,084 = $1,116). This is the income she needs to replace by age 67.

FIGURE 9-4 *Calculating Pensions and Other Income Sources*

The worker is age 50, earns $45,000 annually, and has $25,000 in savings. She wishes to retire at age 67. Her projected monthly Social Security benefit is $1,944. She also has rental income of $600 a month and a pension benefit of $200 a month.

Step 1 Monthly Retirement Income Goal

$45,000 × 22.40 = $1,008,000

$1,008,000 × 0.00417 = $4,200 (rounded)

Step 2 Retirement Monthly Income from Current Savings

$25,000 × 3.261 = $81,525

$81,525 × 0.00417 = $340 (rounded)

Step 3 Monthly Income from Additional Sources

Social Security	$1,944
Pension	200
Rental income	600
Income from current savings	340
	$3,084

Step 4 Required Monthly Savings to Reach Financial Security in Retirement

$4,200
−3,084
$1,116

$1,116 × 0.6029 = $673 (rounded)

The hypothetical worker needs to save $673 a month for 17 years to retire financially secure at age 67.

The worker, by following Step 4, multiplies the Column B factor, next to age 50, in Figure 7-1, by $1,116 (0.6029 × $1,116 = $673). Saving $673 a month for the next 17 years will allow our hypothetical worker to retire and maintain her current standard of living.

FIGURE 9-5 *Review Chart*

Use this chart to determine your retirement savings needs.

Step 1 Monthly Retirement Income Goal

Salary × Age factor (Figure 5-1) = Retirement goal

Retirement goal × 0.00417 = Monthly income goal

Step 2 Retirement Monthly Income from Current Savings

Current savings × years to retirement (Figure 9-1) = Future value

Future value of savings × 0.00417 = Monthly income

Step 3 Monthly Income from Additional Sources

List monthly income from Social Security, pension, rental, etc.

Step 4 Required Monthly Savings to Reach Financial Security in Retirement

Subtract sums from Steps 2 and 3 from Step 1.

Multiply this answer by age factor, Column B, Figure 7-1.

PART THREE

Invest Wisely

CHAPTER 10

A Mind for Investing

If you aren't willing to own a stock for ten years, don't even think about owning it for ten minutes.[1]
Warren Buffett

People save with their hands, but they must invest with their heads. Investing is a mental exercise. A great many people really enjoy investing. They love the intellectual challenge; the risk; the rewards; and the lifetime lessons of discipline, patience, and temperance. Many investors relish the pursuit of new ideas and strategies. Investing for a great many is literally a passionate pursuit. People who are truly passionate about something often bring a great advantage to the table.

There are also a great many people who are completely disinterested in investing. They have absolutely no interest in alpha, beta, delta, or put/call ratios. Capital asset pricing models and modern portfolio and efficient market theories are of absolutely no concern to them. These people would much rather play a round of golf or work in the garden or sit on the porch and leaf through a magazine than worry about "Tobin's q." Ironically enough, those who are completely disinterested in investments and investing bring many advantages to the table as well. In fact, were I to choose which side possessed the greater advantage— those who are passionate about investing or those who hardly care—I'd probably place my money on the totally disinterested, as long as the parties had started now and were saving sufficient sums for retirement.

People who have a tendency to get too lathered up over investments and investing can sometimes do great harm to themselves. It is much like the mechanically minded person who is passionate about working on cars. People who always have their head under a hood often own cars that seldom run. They love cars so much they have a tendency to fix what isn't broken.

People must invest with their heads. This does not mean, however, that one must have an above average IQ to become a successful investor. When it comes to investing, the person with an average IQ can use his or her head just as effectively as the person with an IQ of 160. An average person with average intelligence who is willing to grasp a few simple concepts is likely to do very well with investments.

An Affinity for Common Stocks

If you are not invested in the stock market, it will likely cost you a lot of money over the long term. Further, those who stay away from common stocks will, in all likelihood, fall further and further behind in their retirement savings. People can coexist with all kinds of phobias in life, but those with a mind for investing cannot afford to be afraid of the stock market. The stock market has traditionally been a faithful friend of those who have aspired to become wealthy.

Warren Buffett, as we learned earlier, was born in 1930, less than one year after the crash of 1929. When Buffett began his business career in the 1950s, most people were so terrified of the stock market that bonds actually paid less in interest than common stock dividends. Virtually no one wanted to own common stocks in the 1950s. Conventional wisdom believed that stocks did more to destroy wealth than build it, as memories of the 1929 market crash were still vivid in many minds. Buffett, however, decided to befriend the stock market. It was his belief that a careful analysis of individual securities could uncover some terrific bargains. He, therefore, started from scratch and built an investment partnership that evolved into Berkshire Hathaway. His company is now greater in value than the gross domestic product of the United States in the year he was born. The stock market has historically paid those with a mind for investing well.

The Dow Jones Industrial Average closed around 250 in the year 1950. Fifty-five years later, the Dow stood well above 10,000. This more or less represents an average annual increase of 7.2 percent. Throw in dividends and the Dow has averaged annually about 10.8 percent over the past 50 years. Translated into dollars and cents, a newborn who started life in 1950 with $10,000 in the market at birth would (using 10.8 percent return) be worth more than $2.8 million today. The stock market was exceedingly kind to not only Mr. Buffett, but also to anyone who climbed aboard that train and remained in place for the past 50 years or so.

The famous portfolio manager, Peter Lynch, once said, "[W]hich way the next 1,000 to 2,000 points in the market will go is anybody's guess, but I believe strongly that the next 10,000, 20,000 and 40,000 points will be up."[2] If the Dow Jones Industrial Average grows by just 5.25 percent over the next 50 years, it will close above 125,000 in 2055. If the market mirrors the past 50 years, then 50 years from now it will close above 320,000. I don't know why anyone would want to decline a seat on this bus.

Hersh Shefrin, a professor at Santa Clara University, is an expert in the field of behavioral finance. Shefrin's research indicates the average person is very loathe to the possibility of losing money. Such a phenomenon is called *loss aversion* in the academic community. Citing research performed by Daniel Kahneman and Amos Tversky, a person (psychologically speaking) feels the effect of a loss at a rate of displeasure that is approximately "two and a half times the impact of a gain of the same magnitude."[3] This is the way our brains actually operate. Further, the concept of loss aversion is not just limited to money. It applies to all areas of life. In fact, loss aversion could very well explain why men would prefer to drive around all day lost rather than stop and ask for directions. Apparently, it is a great deal more painful for men to swallow their pride (loss of self-worth) and admit they're lost, than learn how to find their way home (gain of knowledge). Likewise, a person with $100,000 who loses $20,000 will feel two times worse than the pleasure some investor experiences on earning a return of $20,000.

Those who have a mind for overcoming loss aversion have a great advantage when investing. Interestingly, the ability to overcome loss aversion has nothing to do with IQ or intelligence. Loss aversion is tied to emotion. Those with a mind for investing are generally able to keep their emotions under control.

Investing, when one stops to think about it, is a lot like being in love. Those who underestimate the emotional impact of investing will likely be in for a terrible surprise someday. One of my professors at Duke echoed this theme in class one day. "Never be surprised at who people marry or how they spend their money," observed Stuart Henry. Likewise, never be surprised at how people lose money or miss out on great opportunities to make money over time. Investors must understand that emotion and reason are often in competition whenever the mind must make a final judgment on any difficult decision surrounding love or money. The romantic may do very well in love, but when it comes to investing, emotion creates nervous money. "Nervous money," writes Charles Ellis, "never wins."[4]

Nervous money hops around from stock to stock or mutual fund to mutual fund with rapid velocity. When prices drop, nervous money bolts for the exits. When prices go up, nervous money swells with confidence and piles more and more dough into whatever seems to be working. Nervous money is in constant search of hot tips, expert and not-so-expert opinions, and other various forms of flattery. Nervous money is always more than ready to pay homage to the latest stock market prediction or investment guru musing. Nervous money is charged with emotion. It runs with a fast crowd that is forever darting in and out of the market. Nervous money is anxious money.

In contrast to anxious money, Warren Buffett has stated on more than one occasion that whenever he purchases a stock his favorite holding period is "forever."[5] It is Buffett's preference, in other words, to never sell a stock. Robert Hagstrom, a highly successful money manager and long-time student of Warren Buffett and Charlie Munger, conveys the following story on Buffett in his book, *The Essential Buffett.* Melissa Turner, a business writer for the *Atlanta Constitution,* interviewed Buffett shortly after it was revealed in 1989 that Berkshire Hathaway had purchased a sizable stake in the Coca-Cola Company. Buffett explains in this interview how his mind works whenever he purchases a common stock.

Buffett begins by painting a vivid mental picture. Pretend, suggests Buffett, that when you buy a stock you are going to depart on a long trip lasting 10 long years. Once you make a decision to purchase a security, that choice is irreversible for a decade. Given those parameters, there are at least three things you would want to seriously consider. First, the business would have to be "simple and understandable." Second, the business would have to have a long track record of consistency. Third, the future "long-term prospects would have to be favorable."[6] Considering these three business characteristics, Buffett said he couldn't think of a better investment in 1989 than Coke. "I'd be relatively sure that when I came back they would be doing a hell of a lot more business than they do now."[7] It has been nearly 17 years since that interview, and Berkshire still owns Coke.

Viewing an investment opportunity from a long-term perspective of 10 years tends to wring the emotion out of a decision. A decade-long commitment makes day-to-day fluctuations in price insignificant. Buffett's investment methodology effectively circumvents the emotional aspect. For example, buy companies with easy-to-understand business models, advises Buffett. His advice is helpful because, if something goes wrong, you'll at least have some idea of the underlying dynamics. In fact, instead of hitting the panic button, you'll probably want to buy more shares when prices drop. Understanding a simple business model facilitates the use of reason over emotion. Second, make sure your investments have a long history of success. Good strong businesses are often inclined to bring investors many positive surprises. And finally, buy companies whose products or services are widely recognized and in demand. Coca-Cola is one of the world's most recognizable names. In 1989, as you may recall, the Iron Curtain fell. This opened the rest of the world's markets for one of the most prominent business names in the known universe. Quarterly earnings numbers are of little importance when you can be sure that 10 years from now a company will be making a lot more money. Buffett's decision-making process, from my perspective, eliminates most of the emotional issues before the commitment to deploy capital is ever made.

To illustrate further how ordinary investors can develop their methodology for effectively managing emotion, Robert Hagstrom suggests a second model that was developed by Warren Buffett.[8] Imagine, suggests Buffett, that as an investor you have a card with only 20 punches in it. The card must last for a single lifetime, meaning that a person will only get the opportunity to make 20 security purchases over the entirety of one's life. The point is straightforward. People who use the cards will likely be exceedingly careful with their investment choices. In fact, if the purchases are rationed over one's adult lifetime, that person could make a purchase once every two years. This gives the investor plenty of time to plot any potential buys very carefully. A person under this scenario would be unlikely to ever commit funds to an investment unless that person was highly certain the security would perform well over the remainder of one's lifetime. Putting the brakes on frequent investment decisions is a practical way to eliminate anxious money.

People who save and invest for retirement should be able to comfortably focus attention on the attainment of long-term results. The stock market, interestingly enough, is exceedingly predictable over long-term time horizons. It is much like a person who is farsighted. Whenever a person is farsighted, that person has trouble seeing objects that are in close range. Everything up close is fuzzy. Objects that are far away, however, can be seen in precise detail. That is how the market operates. Nobody knows, for instance, what the market will do tomorrow. It is anyone's guess. Looking one year out, the market is still mysteriously uncertain. Again, no one knows whether the market will be up or down or flat over the next 12 months. Ten years from now, markets will begin to reveal some focus. There is an 80 percent chance stocks will outperform bonds and cash. Twenty years from now, the odds improve to 90 percent. At 30 years, it is almost certain that stocks will surpass the performance of bonds and cash.[9] The pattern is clear. Over the long-term, stocks have been fairly reliable investments. When viewed from a short-term perspective, however, the market appears chaotic and uncertain. That is perhaps one reason Warren Buffett says his favorite holding period is forever. The markets traditionally reward handsomely those with a long-term approach to investing.

Different Paths, Same Goal

Warren Buffett buys individual stocks. He manages emotion by taking a long-term view of the markets and carefully analyzing security purchases. His exceedingly rare ability to analyze individual companies on financial, business, and strategic terms gives him a tremendous advantage over others. Without the ability to perform in-depth financial analysis, most individual investors are going to be at a great disadvantage when selecting individual stocks. The inability to perform adequate financial analysis on individual securities often creates nervous money for people. Thus, when prices fall investors have a tendency to panic because they cannot fully evaluate the underlying business dynamics. The emotional pain intensifies as the loss of money increases with each downward spike in price. When the emotional toll is intolerable, people cease investing.

The attainment of long-term financial goals is the trademark of investing wisely. All investors, both the interested and disinterested, must be able to follow a common path that leads to the same destination at retirement. Buying and selling individual securities with retirement dollars is not a path the overwhelming majority of investors should try to travel. Those without the background, ability, and time to analyze corporate balance sheets and income statements will usually find themselves gravely disappointed. The results at retirement, needless to say, will be mixed.

Two finance professors at the University of Notre Dame, George M. Korniotis and Alok Kumar, authored an academic working paper in which they studied stock holdings and trades from more than 75,000 individual accounts. Their research focused on the relationship between investment performance and various age groups. These scholars discovered, not surprisingly, that "every age group in their study trailed the market."[10] It is exceedingly difficult, as mentioned earlier, for average investors to outperform the market averages.

Those without the ability to analyze businesses, according to Warren Buffett, should buy index funds. One such index fund is the S&P 500. This particular index is comprised of 500 companies that represent some of America's largest and best-known firms. Such a broadly diversified universe of common stocks serves both the interested and disinterested investor equally well. It requires absolutely zero business skill to purchase shares in an S&P 500 index fund. And as discussed earlier, the S&P 500 will experience periods in which it will outperform the majority of professional investors. An index fund of this caliber makes tremendous sense over the long term.

The S&P 500 is put together by a selection committee that looks for companies representing the overall U.S. economy. Companies selected have generally been around for some time, are often leaders in their respective fields, and are projected to survive for at least 10 years or more. Further, companies in the S&P 500 represent basically all sectors of the U.S. economy, such as manufacturing, retail, pharmaceutical, chemical, aerospace, technology, and entertainment. The S&P 500 is therefore a proxy for American business in general. Those who have confidence that the American economy will continue to thrive going forward well into the 21st century can confidently place long-term retirement money in a fund that imitates the S&P 500.

An investment such as the S&P 500 addresses and answers the three questions posed by Warren Buffett when he purchased Coca-Cola back in 1989. First, an S&P 500 index fund is an investment that is easy to understand. Second, it has a strong and reliable record of success. And finally, the prospects of going forward should continue to favorably mirror the strength of the American economy. Few people, to date, have ever been disappointed when betting on American business prospects.

Investors saving for retirement have also experienced a great deal of success investing in mutual funds with impressive long-term records of solid performance. Some mutual funds date all the way back to the 1920s. A mutual fund, as you may recall, purchases shares of common stock across a broad array of different companies. Investors who buy shares in a mutual fund therefore own company stock in a variety of industries. Mutual funds, like an index fund such as the S&P 500, are generally widely diversified investments. They are often ideal investments for ordinary savers who lack the financial and business acumen to expertly analyze the securities of individual companies. Mutual funds have made countless individuals wealthy. A great many millionaires in the United States attribute their wealth to mutual fund investments.

Broadly diversified mutual funds are investments that can serve workers well for a lifetime. A portfolio of carefully selected mutual funds that includes various asset classes can provide investors with a sure-footed way to build retirement wealth. Further, those who participate in 401(k)s or other corporate-sponsored retirement programs often qualify to receive preferential pricing on mutual fund share purchases. Deferring savings into professionally managed mutual funds allows even those who are disinterested in investing to confidently prepare and save for retirement.

There are many ways to invest wisely. Fortunately, it does not require the rare gifts of a Warren Buffett or Charlie Munger to become wealthy by retirement age. Ordinary workers with average or even below average investment aptitude can do just fine. Key, however, is the acknowledgment of one's limitations. People, especially those with a passion for investing, must realize that it is highly improbable to outperform the market averages when one is an average investor. Index funds and a great many professionally managed mutual funds are proven vehicles of wealth creation with long and fully documented records of success. Those who are unafraid of normal returns and comfortable with *forever* as an investment time horizon are more than able to invest wisely.

CHAPTER 11

Getting an Edge
in the Market

You have to start with some ideas about reality.[1]
Charlie Munger

Amateurs and Professionals

Several years ago when I worked in Chicago there was a guy with an office down the hall from me who owned a professional baseball team. Sometimes after work I would stop by his office and chat for a while before heading home. One evening I asked him a question: "Do major leaguers run faster or hit farther or throw harder than minor league players?"

"No, not really," he answered.

"Then what is the key difference between minor league and major league players?"

"Consistency," he responded. "A major leaguer is going to get it right nearly every time. They've had years and years to practice getting it right."

Unlike professional baseball players, average workers get only one shot at preparing for retirement. They must do so as amateurs. It takes investors 30 or 40 years to accumulate enough wealth for retirement. Starting from scratch and becoming financially independent takes a full, working lifetime for most people. Wealth creation is not something that you can just practice and practice and practice and then finally figure out on your 60th birthday. Those who work and save for retirement must understand that wealth creation for the vast majority is done as an amateur, meaning serious mistakes can spoil the whole process. The path of financial independence is a serious one because most will only travel this road once.

Harry S. Truman was the 33rd President of the United States. His father was John Truman. John Truman was a hard-nosed and feisty pioneer who lived in Missouri. He was a tough man who believed much could be attained through courage and determination. John Truman started from nothing and made a living trading livestock. An astute trader, he eventually began to accumulate meaningful wealth. By the time Harry Truman was in high school, his family had acquired a prestigious address in Independence. Inside the house there were books, a Kimball piano, and $40,000 in savings. Life was comfortable for the Trumans in the year 1900.

Truman's father, who was a very successful horse trader, then shifted wealth strategies. He started trading grain futures—where the real money was being made. Unfortunately, he fell victim to an amateurish investment mistake. He became overconfident and failed to think through the implications of taking on more risk. Those who try to accelerate the wealth creation process by overreaching can lose everything. By 1901, he was broke. The Truman family lost their home, 160 acres in farmland, and the $40,000 in savings. John Truman, at age 51, was walking the streets looking for work. He ended up working as a night watchman at the grain elevators. He never recovered his wealth.[2] This story illustrates why people must be so careful. There is no time for practice; financial independence is a road traveled only once in life.

William Miller is one of the best portfolio managers in the country. He consistently outperforms the S&P 500. Miller once remarked that investors are prone to make common errors. People, as a rule, tend to suffer from "overconfidence, overreaction, loss aversion, mental accounting, magical thinking, false patterns, and crowd psychology."[3] The mistakes investors make today are the very same ones that have been made for centuries. Unfortunately, these mistakes, although universal in nature, are not benign. Overconfidence, overreaction, and magical thinking can wipe people out financially. These serious errors are deadly; these errors are common missteps for amateur investors.

Harry Truman, reflecting on his father's catastrophic missteps, once said, "He got the notion he could get rich."[4] Truman's dad succumbed to overconfidence and started taking on too much risk. When he started losing money, he suffered from overreaction. He compounded his mistake by trying to break even. He spiraled helplessly down the drain by magically thinking he could escape disaster by taking on even more risk. Charles Ellis, writing in his book, *Winning the Loser's Game,* notes, "The greatest secret for success in long-term investing is to avoid serious losses."[5] People who start from nothing get one working lifetime to become financially independent. Time is only able to pardon a finite number of errors; simply staying away from foolish mistakes helps maximize savings in a very real way.

One other overlooked impression that ruins people is the mistaken belief that one must outperform others to get an edge in the markets. It is anxious money, however, that generally gets taken for a ride when chasing after performance. The message of this book is that average investment returns get the job done just fine. The normal growth of money, as explained in Chapter 4, is more than sufficient to satisfy long-term personal retirement goals.

Amateur investors who work with a financial professional, from my perspective, enjoy an incredible advantage over those who choose to go it alone. True financial professionals specialize in the proven concepts of wealth creation. They are actively engaged over and over again with their clients in the lifetime process of personal financial accumulation. Their results are consistent. In addition, they are well able to identify the subtle nuances of overconfidence, overreaction, and magical thinking. Generally a few paces ahead of the ordinary investor, they are able to skillfully steer one away from mistakes that result in serious losses.

Once one has decided to partner with a financial professional, there are certain expectations that person is welcome to bring to the table. First, there should be an ongoing dialogue. The context for dialogue between the amateur investor and financial professional should ideally start with a financial goal for retirement. Personal timetables and investment selections should be quantified and defined. Professionals are most helpful when they enable investors to identify the boundaries of investment propriety and then encourage them to remain within those prescribed parameters. Staying far away from dangers that can destroy savings is one way for individuals to prosper when investing. Individuals cognizant of their amateur status truly have an edge in the financial markets, especially when they have good relationships with a financial professional able to protect them from harm.

Partner with the IRS

Taxes are a consequence of prosperity. Those who make money in America pay taxes. Taxes are a fact of life. No adult citizen gets to keep everything earned. The government, in a sense, is one's business partner. That means every great corporation as well as each individual who collects a paycheck partners with the IRS. One doesn't even have to be particularly good at business or earn especially high wages. The government does not discriminate when it comes to taxes. The rules are simple: The government is supposed to get paid whenever money is being created.

I have studied business models for many years. To date, I have not yet discovered a more attractive business than the IRS. Their scope of revenue is just simply incredible. For instance, take payroll taxes. Everyone in America who has a job is supposed to pay taxes. The very first cent of every legal paycheck drawn in America goes to the IRS. More than 150 million workers will get paid this month, but will take home only what is left after the IRS gets its cut. Warren Buffett and Charlie Munger have owned some great companies over the years, but none, including Berkshire Hathaway, can match that kind of market share. The IRS has 100 percent of the market. And what about competitors? Forget it! Those who compete with the IRS and get caught go to the big house. There are some absolutely fantastic companies in the United States, but none are allowed to discourage competition by sending competitors to jail. Then there is the whole matter of customer service. I have not once heard or read about the government ever calling valued customers, like some well-heeled billionaires, and thanking them for once again sending in millions of tax dollars. One would think the IRS would like to show some gratitude every now and then by letting a few of these big shots take a ride on the space shuttle or borrow an F-16 for a weekend or work out a time share with the White House some summer. Instead, the government, to my knowledge, does absolutely nothing to soften the blow for handing over all that money.

The government does, however, take its role as a fellow business partner seriously. It makes sure the air, seaways, rails, and highways are reasonably safe and in good working order for the transport and trade of goods. The government tries to keep world markets open and fair. Corrupt or unreasonable labor practices are forbidden. Access to utilities is available to all cities and states. The Army, Navy, Air Force, and Coast

Guard protect our borders and foreign interests from invasion or sub-version. Commerce, under the watchful eye of good government, main-tains a playing field that is more or less inviting and equitable. The government and IRS are not perfect, but they do want Americans to suc-ceed. Those fortunate enough to be born in the United States possess a wonderful advantage over the rest of the world when it comes to the cre-ation of individual wealth.

The IRS is particularly eager to partner with those who wish to be-come wealthy by retirement age. There are a variety of government-approved savings vehicles that offer private citizens and public workers great tax advantages for retirement savings. Individual Retirement Ac-counts (IRAs), 401(k)s, 403(b)s, 457s, and other savings programs are all basically designed to give individuals an extra edge by trimming the tax bill on investment savings and earnings. The less money a person pays in taxes, the more one is able to generate in wealth. Government retire-ment savings programs offer individuals at least four ways to reduce fed-eral tax obligations when saving and building wealth. Those able to identify and profit from these four special tax incentives gain an impor-tant edge in the markets.

All workers who save for retirement are generally eligible to qualify for tax deductions when they put money away into special retirement ac-counts, such as 401(k), IRA, or 403(b) plans. Tax deductions are perhaps best understood as a form of government subsidy. Let's assume that your tax bracket is 20 percent. You decide this year to save $5,000 in your 401(k) at work. The government will allow you to reduce your an-nual tax bill by 20 percent of whatever you decide to save. For example, $5,000 in savings multiplied by 20 percent will reduce your annual taxes by $1,000. If you then save the $1,000 in tax savings, in addition to the $5,000 already budgeted, you would receive an edge in the market of $1,000, compliments of the IRS.

Some workers qualify for tax credits. These are usually lower-paid workers. A tax credit is the same thing as free cash. This is how it works: Let's say a worker owes $1,000 in federal income taxes, but because of annual wage limitations, qualifies for a tax credit. If this person were to put $1,000 into an IRA, the tax bill would be reduced to zero. All work-ers who qualify for tax credits and owe federal income taxes have an easy choice to make. Either pay the IRS or cancel the tax bill and pay them-selves instead. Free money is a great way to get an edge in the market.

One should make sure, before ever paying taxes, he or she checks to see if retirement savings tax credits apply. When the government hands out free money, it always makes sense to take it.

The earnings in government-qualified retirement accounts, such as 401(k), IRA, and 403(b) plans, are nearly always tax deferred. This means investors are not required to pay taxes on any of the earnings until the money is withdrawn or taken out of the account. Deferring taxes is usually a benefit to the individual saver. Let's take a look at an example. Two people plan to save $5,000 a year. Both will earn 7.2 percent a year. The tax rate will be an identical 25 percent for both workers. One person decides to pay taxes each year on the earnings. The other person chooses to defer paying taxes on the investment earnings until some future date. Over the next 40 years both workers will put away a total of $200,000. The first person, by paying taxes each year, will have given the IRS a total of $167,439 at the end of 40 years. He will have $702,318 in total after-tax savings. The second person, who deferred paying taxes, will have a total of $1,126,778. She is a millionaire. The IRS will now collect taxes as she withdraws the proceeds as annual income. Should the full $1,126,778 get immediately taxed at the same 25 percent rate, she will still have $140,000 more than the person who did not defer taxes. It generally makes sense to partner with the IRS when given the opportunity to defer taxes.

Current IRS regulations allow some IRAs and 401(k)s to participate in what is called a special Roth provision. These retirement accounts typically do not offer an up-front tax deduction, but do allow the earnings to accrue on a tax-deferred basis. At retirement age the money in these accounts can be withdrawn completely tax-free. For example, had the second person in the preceding example on deferring taxes elected to save for retirement in a special after-tax Roth account, the full $1.1 million would be completely tax free.

It is a mistake to view the IRS as an adversary when building retirement wealth. The wise partner closely with the government whenever possible. The smart ones know that certain tax deductions, tax credits, and tax deferrals divert money away from the government and into the pockets of those who participate in qualified retirement programs. Astute investors are usually quick to recognize any opportunity that offers someone an edge in the market. When the world's absolute best business model offers an opportunity to partner, accept!

Prepare for Panics

Sir John Templeton is recognized throughout the United States as an extraordinary investor. After growing up in Tennessee and paying his way through college at Yale, he went to Wall Street in the 1930s. Pessimism during the Great Depression was pronounced and widespread. Then in 1939, the outlook grew even darker when Germany invaded Poland. The world's predicament, feared many, was getting worse and worse. Templeton, however, had a plan. He called his broker and put $100 into every stock listed on both the New York and American stock exchanges that was selling for less than $1. All in all, he purchased 104 different companies; 34 of these companies were bankrupt and selling for just pennies per share.[6] Within four years, Templeton had made a small fortune. He was on his way to becoming one of the greatest professional money managers in the country.

As discussed earlier, no one knows what the market will do tomorrow or the next day or the next year. Most can be reasonably certain, though, that before their investing days are finished, there will be a panic in the markets, even, perhaps, several panics. Those who are prepared for these inevitable meltdowns will most likely have an edge in the market. It pays, literally, to prepare for the worst.

Workers who invest in 401(k) plans are often asked about their tolerance for risk. These surveys question whether people consider themselves to be aggressive, moderate, or conservative investors. Sometimes the questionnaires will probe even deeper into one's perceived investment tolerances. For instance, some surveys inquire as to how one would anticipate behaving should the market drop by 5, 15, or 25 percent. Although well intentioned, these surveys are of little value. When the markets get really routed, it is just not the conservative investors who panic. The aggressive ones stampede for the exits as well. When fire breaks out in a dark theatre, no one can predict the outcome of events likely to unfold.

Charlie Munger is impressed with how airline pilots are trained.[7] Pilots spend an inordinate number of hours in flight simulators preparing for every type of emergency imaginable. The airlines understand exceedingly well the unpredictable nature of panic situations. Pilots are therefore continually trained to expect the unexpected. Whenever the unanticipated breaks out in flight, good pilots are already five steps ahead mentally.

Imagine, for example, that you are sitting in a commercial aircraft 40,000 feet above the earth and traveling at a speed of 400 mph. Suddenly, the jetliner gets into trouble. It is a panic situation, wherein the plane could go down. Now ask yourself, "Does it matter whether the pilot is an aggressive or conservative aviator?" Trying to discover a solution by measuring someone's risk preference under such extreme circumstances is hardly relevant. The question is not whether the pilot is a barnstormer or an FAA compliance officer, but rather, does he or she have the ability to execute a proven plan in the midst of a panic situation? It is precisely the same when investing. It is illogical to try and manage investment risk by accommodating temperament. When you truly know what you're doing in a panic situation, risk is minimized.

Sir John Templeton had little wealth in 1939, but he had a plan. When share prices were collapsing in the markets, Templeton took some money and bought what were believed to be the most beaten-down stocks listed on both major stock exchanges. A near-complete absence of optimism caused people to unload shares for mere pennies. Investors in 1939 had suffered enough. Many just wanted out. Price no longer mattered. Reason was subordinate to the fear that more horrible news was imminent.

Thoughtful investors are like professional pilots in that both are prepared with a plan for the inevitable day of panic. The issue is not about perceived impressions of one's investing temperament, but rather, the plan for panic. When people were panicked in the 1930s, Sir John Templeton was prepared with a plan. This edge allowed him to make a small fortune. Once, when the markets were weak and people were bailing out in the early 1970s, Warren Buffett was boldly building positions that would eventually make him and many of his shareholders millions. He was as cool as a cucumber. He knew exactly what he was doing and what he wanted to buy. He had a plan for panic.

There are several ways investors can prepare for panics with a plan. First, one must not be naive. Understand fully that a panic is someday likely to occur. One should not be fooled into believing that one will see it coming and be able to pull off an escape. Panics always come out of nowhere. Even seasoned investors get caught off guard. No one outsmarts the market. Expect, like everyone else, to get surprised. That is the first step in planning.

Second, refrain from borrowing money to purchase securities. Sometimes brokerage firms will allow you to purchase securities on margin, which is, in fact, a loan. These loans can work well when markets are marching upward, but when markets fall, you can literally lose everything. When you own your securities outright, you can always wait for prices to recover. If you own securities on margin, the securities are sometimes called away to meet margin requirements. This means you will be forced to sell at prices that are generally unfavorable. Charlie Munger once said, "Warren and I are chicken about buying stocks on margin. There's always a slight chance of catastrophe when you own securities pledged to others."[8] Plan well for panics. Never put yourself in a situation in which you can lose everything. Respect the markets.

Third, stay away from securities than can fall to zero. Options, futures contracts, and low-priced stocks that sell for less than $5 a share can become worthless. These investments are very speculative. Many institutions, for instance, are not permitted to own stocks that list for prices less than $5 a share. Individual investors, when buying speculative stocks, should not consider themselves smarter than institutions. Options and futures are also full of danger. Option contracts expire within a certain period of time, ranging from days to sometimes years. If the markets move against you and time runs out, your investment can go to zero with no chance of recovery. Your loss will be equal to 100 percent of your investment. Option contracts as well as futures require you to guess correctly within a predetermined time period.

Fourth, make sure you understand the securities in your portfolio. Own such securities that, should the market tumble, you will buy even more shares at the lower prices. Think in terms of accumulating more and more shares. Learn to focus, not on whether prices are moving up, but rather on the number of additional shares you can purchase whenever prices fall. For example, prosperous farmers are often on the lookout for more acreage at bargain basement prices. Farmers understand the potential value of land. When prices fall, farmers are inclined to buy more and more land at lower prices. Those who have no idea of what it is they own are most likely to panic. Know your investments as well as a farmer understands farmland, and if you do not understand any potential investment this well, hold on to your money.

Finally, always try to keep a little extra cash on hand. Cash is a great thing to own when stock prices are falling. A lack of cash reserves is one of the most common errors investors tend to make. Cash should play a role in every investor's plan for panic. When people are panicking, prices are cheap, and cash gives investors a ready edge in the market.

Make sure you and your financial professional always have a plan in place for panics. Anticipate the unexpected. Don't get fooled by market emotion. Insulate yourself from harm by refusing to buy securities on margin or owning those that can go to zero. Understand what you own, and be prepared to buy more of what you already own when prices fall. Always keep a little cash safely tucked away, just in case. And think back every now and then to Sir John Templeton, Warren Buffett, and Charlie Munger. These men are all much, much wealthier today, not because stock prices never dropped precipitously, but because they were prepared with a plan. Prepare for panic.

CHAPTER 12

The Irony of Making Money

This is the one thing I can never understand. When stocks go down and
you can get more for your money, people don't like them anymore.
Warren Buffett

Behind the News

Most readers can probably recall a time when the stock market fell precipitously. Prices fell like raindrops in a monsoon. Bad news just kept pouring and pouring down. There was no respite anywhere. Newspapers were full of concern, if not outright terror. All the stories highlighted people losing money. The television financial news shows were just as shrill. The anchors all looked worn and edgy and tired. The on-air guests, namely, financial experts, were respectfully sober. "Folks, this is just the beginning," an expert was likely to have predicted. "Unfortunately, there is more bad news to come. I'm anticipating the market to drop another 1,000, maybe even 2,500, points before we begin to see some support. This bear is an ugly one."

When prices are falling steeply, the thing that is sometimes so distressing for individual investors who must watch the news from home or work is the suspicion that those in the crowd know something the general public does not. How else, many are prone to think, can the abrupt drop in prices be explained? When prices fall below normal expectations, there is always an extra measure of apprehension regarding who knows what. People therefore turn to their televisions, radios, computers, and newspapers in search of the real story.

Surprisingly, the real story is generally right there on the air or in print. The story can be taken, in other words, at face value. The people on television or in the newspapers don't know a thing more about the fall in prices than the typical viewer who is watching the whole story unfold at home. The media knows, principally, what everybody else already knows. Prices are falling. That, by the way, is the meaning of *conventional thought:* It is what everybody else already knows. Most of the experts who get paraded out in front of the cameras or get quoted in the newspapers all sing in perfect pitch from the same hymnal of conventional wisdom.

There are basically two things you'll never get to see during a television news story reporting lower stock prices. First, you'll never get to see the expert guest grab his cell phone and call his girlfriend immediately after the broadcast and solicit her compliments. Ralph Wanger, the legendary portfolio manager of the Acorn Fund, once made this observation in his excellent book, *A Zebra in Lion Country.* Wanger points out that when prices either go up or go down, people figure there must be a reason the markets moved. A reporter, therefore, calls a Wall Street bond desk and gets some trader on the phone. The trader has no idea why rates are off, but he figures his name in the paper will impress his girlfriend. So, the trader looks at his terminal and makes up some story that sounds reasonable.[1] Ever since reading Wanger's analysis, I always try to frame expert opinions from the perspective of "who is this person *really* trying to impress?" What people have to understand is that the media's interests are not always going to be aligned with the individual investor's priorities. Those in the media, whether in print or on the air, are paid to convey stories in the most accurate, yet captivating, way possible. It is their job to keep readers or viewers interested in the story, which is why bad news sometimes gets exaggerated and good news promoted with a great deal of enthusiasm. When prices are falling, the story usually covers the pain of losing money in some fashion. Conversely, when prices are shooting higher, there is often a bias toward the euphoria of making lots of money.

The second, and more important, thing you'll never get to see is what the smart money is doing while you watch the stock market meltdown on television. Smart money is quiet money. Brilliance has a tendency to counter conventional thinking. The flow of smart money is a story that nearly always lies hidden from the general public. Those who write in the papers and report on camera do not get paid to manage your investments. The chances are good that little will be said or written that will have much of an impact on you. That is one reason Warren Buffett keeps the sound turned off on his television when he is in the office.

Money is made whenever people buy securities at low prices and then sell at higher prices. This is smart money. It is a story that could really help people who must save and invest for retirement. Unfortunately, the story of smart money is seldom ever reported when prices are falling, as the media has a tendency to get all tangled up in conventional thought. Strangely, the buyers, when things look really dismal, often escape notice. Smart money is conspicuously absent when the crowds are huddled at the exits.

"This is the one thing I can never understand," said Buffett once. "When stocks go down and you can get more for your money, people don't like them anymore."[2] For example, were a store owner to mark down television prices by 20 percent on the day after Thanksgiving, crowds would literally stream into the store on Friday morning. Some customers might even camp out all night so as to not miss the sale. Mark down the stock market by 20 percent, however, and people stampede away from the sale. They instead head for the exits, convinced the world is about to end. It is one of the great ironies of making money.

Individual investors who wish to emulate smart money must condition themselves to execute three very important tasks whenever prices are falling. First, they must buy stocks when prices go on sale. Falling prices are not necessarily cause for panic; falling prices are often reason for celebration. Second, investors must understand exactly what they own. People are generally prone to panic whenever prices collapse and they have no idea what it is they own. Consumers will buy television sets when there is a sale, because people understand the worth of a new television that comes with a 12-month warranty. An investor is not likely to hold onto a security when the price plummets if that person thinks there is a reasonable chance of losing significant sums of money. Third, people must own securities that are unlikely to ever go all the way to zero. Those who are reasonably confident that their portfolios will never become completely worthless can buy all the way down with the full expectation of someday making money.

Mitigating Risk

It is always a good idea to put new thoughts to the test. It was stated earlier that individual investors should own investments they understand and that won't go to zero. Once a person discovers such an investment, then the ideal time to purchase it is when the price is going down. Prices in the stock market that fall in value are analogous to a sale at a retail store. The lower the price, the more goods one is able to purchase. This is a classic example of how smart money works.

Finding a security that will not become worthless is the first step to executing a smart money strategy. It makes sense to begin this search by first looking at the largest, most established, blue-chip companies in the country. These companies would include names such as General Electric, ExxonMobil, Microsoft, and Citigroup. These stalwarts are well-known giants of commerce and, in many ways, support the backbone of our U.S. economy by providing leadership in energy, manufacturing, technology, and finance.

When one's initial objective is to avoid the possibility of getting wiped out, it makes little sense to make a single bet on any one of these outstanding companies. The world, as we well know, can and will change over time. There are myriad ways companies, even great companies, can step on a rake and get into serious trouble. For example, there have been extreme cases of companies getting into difficulty with product liability issues, labor troubles, industrial accidents, fraudulent executive behavior, obsolete business strategies, or any number of other completely unforeseen predicaments. Although it would be highly, highly improbable, it would not be impossible for a single great company to implode. A person should think long and hard before investing the entirety of one's retirement nest egg in a single stock.

An obvious way to mitigate the risk of losing all of one's money by investing in a single, large, well-established, blue-chip company is to divide the dollars among a host of large, well-established, blue-chip companies. The more one splits his or her money among large, well-established companies, the greater the probability that one will not lose everything in the event of a disastrous market meltdown. That is one of the most important strategic aspects of investing in a mutual fund. Mutual funds diversify the risk of losing everything by spreading investment dollars among a broad array of different companies. An S&P 500 index fund, for example, spreads one's investment dollars across 500 of the country's largest companies. Many mutual funds that invest in large, well-established, blue-chip companies will typically own anywhere from 50 to 100 different stocks.

Those who invest in either an S&P 500 index fund or mutual fund comprised of large, well-established companies are essentially transferring the risk of owning separate companies to the anticipated well-being and strength of the U.S. economy. In other words, the U.S. economy would basically have to vanish, dissipate, or self-destruct in order for an S&P 500 index fund or high-quality, large capitalization (large, well-established, blue-chip companies) mutual fund to become worthless. By placing money in an S&P 500 index fund or large cap mutual fund, an investor is basically placing his or her confidence in the vibrancy and innovation and supremacy of the U.S. economy. Investors, as noted earlier, have traditionally done very well by trusting and investing in America's future economic prospects.

There are also extra safeguards to further protect the individual when investing in either an index fund or mutual fund. As mentioned earlier, mutual funds are diversified investments, meaning these funds are generally not permitted to have more than 5 percent of their total assets in a single stock or security. Mutual funds, by law, must be diversified among a wide variety of different securities. There are also certain statutory restrictions. Regulations make it basically impractical for mutual funds to either short (borrow) stock or create leverage (buy on margin). Exposure to obligations beyond a fund's assets is not permitted. Additionally, individuals who operate mutual funds must report to a board of directors. The primary responsibility of the board is to make certain mutual funds serve the interests of shareholders. Finally, mutual funds carry fidelity bonds, which are insurance vehicles that protect investors against fraud.

The reasons for owning broadly diversified large capitalization mutual funds are at least twofold. First, these types of investments are easy for investors to understand. When investors know what they own, they are less prone to panic and run for the exits when prices fall. Second, it is highly improbable that any large cap index fund or well-diversified, large cap mutual fund would ever fall to zero and become completely worthless. When investors know what they own and can maintain confidence that their investments will not fall to zero, they can then confidently purchase more shares at lower prices. Holding steady and buying more shares while others are fearful and dumping their holdings at bargain-basement prices is how smart money operates in the market. Owning large cap mutual funds gives ordinary investors a tremendous advantage in the stock market. These types of investments enable workers to invest like seasoned professionals whenever stock prices go on sale.

Come Hell or High Water
(A Hypothetical Story of Falling Stock Prices)

A volunteer, eager to try his hand at emulating smart money, agreed to invest money every month into a reputable large cap mutual fund with an excellent track record. The fund was understood well by this investor. The money would be spread among 70 to 80 large, well-established, blue-chip companies. It should not fall to zero or become completely worthless unless something horrendous were to happen, like the national economy collapsing. The investor agreed to invest $1,000 a month into the fund for 12 consecutive months. He would initiate the program in January and evaluate his progress at the end of December. The investor was so confident he pledged in advance to stay with his prescribed plan "come hell or high water."

When the first day of January rolled around, our fearless volunteer stepped up to the plate and invested $1,000 into the mutual fund. Each share was selling to the public for $10 a share. The investor therefore bought a total of 100 shares. This, as luck would have it, was the high water mark.

By the time February came, all hell had broken loose in the markets. Stocks had plummeted. The situation was far, far worse than even the experts could imagine. In fact, no one interviewed either on television or in the newspapers could ever recall such a precipitous market collapse. The fearless volunteer's mutual fund shares had fallen all the way to 50¢ per share. His initial $1,000 investment was now worth only $50. Nobody appeared to be buying stock. Everyone, reported the news shows, was getting out of the market. It was even reported that the chairman of the Federal Reserve was buying Treasury bills. The volunteer, however, remained true to his word. He invested another $1,000 in the market. It was one of the toughest decisions he had ever made. He now owned 2,100 shares.

March was no better. Stocks had failed to recover. Everyone, it seemed, was selling. No one appeared to be buying. The times were just too uncertain. Some people were saying that it could take 100 years for this thing to straighten itself out. The volunteer remained steadfast to his pledge. Although he felt like he was throwing hard-earned money away, he put another $1,000 into the market. He now owned 4,100 shares. The price was still at rock bottom levels of 0.50¢ a share.

There was a rumor in April that stocks would move up once everyone made their annual IRA contributions by April 15. Unfortunately, there was no merit to the rumor. Nothing could move this market. Our nervous volunteer decided to call his financial advisor. The volunteer confessed that he never figured things would ever get this bad. He asked the financial professional whether it would make sense to cut back on the $1,000 monthly contributions. The advisor, however, was a real professional. He had been through difficult times over and over again in his career. The advisor counseled the volunteer to hold fast and stick with the plan. "Stocks are on sale. Keep buying!" Our volunteer swallowed hard and threw another $1,000 into the mutual fund that was proving to be so disappointing. His investment after only one month had fallen in price by 95 percent. It was still just barely hanging in there at 0.50¢ a share. He now owned 6,100 shares.

May, June, July, August, and September were all like February, March, and April. The news was mostly bad. The mutual fund just couldn't budge. Absolutely no one, it seemed, wanted to buy stocks. Without buyers, there was hardly any hope for a market recovery. People were advised to stay away from the stock market. Conventional wisdom believed that ordinary investors should refrain from trading shares until after the November elections. The volunteer kept investing. At the end of September, he owned 16,100 shares. The price, however, was still 95 percent off the January high.

October brought good news. People were expecting the worst, since October is always rumored to be such a bad month for the market. Instead, prices recovered a little and went up some. The experts were calling it a "dead cat bounce." Investors were strongly advised to not fall for the modest rise in prices. It was declared a "head fake." The volunteer dumped another $1,000 into the mutual fund. The fund was now selling for $1 a share. He was still down from his original price by 90 percent.

November and December were good months. The market continued to improve some in November and a little more in December. By the end of the year the investor's mutual fund had risen all the way to $2 a share. All in all, it had been one of the most difficult years ever for the investor. He bought a mutual fund for $10 dollars a share in January and the fund had lost 80 percent of its value by December. It was the worst year ever for the stock market.

Remarkably, the volunteer could hardly believe his eyes when he studied his year-end mutual fund statement. He had invested a total of $12,000 or $1,000 a month for 12 months. His fund, as stated, had dropped in value by $8 a share, or 80 percent. He now owned 18,266 shares. His account was worth $36,352. He had tripled his money in what was supposed to have been the worst year ever for stocks. The results were just absolutely incredible. He was up more than 200 percent in a single year.

Interestingly, no one from the newspapers or financial news shows ever called him for an interview. Smart money, remember, is quiet money. Even though the headlines usually articulate conventional thought accurately, the real story of smart money is often underreported. Those with investment savvy were scooping up shares while the public was frantically dumping.

The lesson is worth repeating. Understand what it is that you own. Hold securities that won't fall to zero. And when prices are falling, buy more. That is irony of making money.

Falling Prices Benefit Buyers

Many readers are surprised to learn that it is possible to earn a return of more than 200 percent within a single year even though prices have collapsed by 80 percent. While it is true that prices eventually have to move upward to make money, prices do not necessarily have to exceed one's initial purchase price as long as an investor continues to purchase additional shares at the lower prices. The eager volunteer earned phenomenal returns because he was able to purchase 20 times as many shares with subsequent dollars due to the collapse in prices from $10 a

share to 0.50¢ a share. Should the eager volunteer's investment ever return to the original price of $10 a share, the initial investment consisting
of $12,000 and 18,266 shares would be worth $182,660. The point is a
very simple one. When prices fall, investors who are accumulating
wealth are able to buy more shares for the same dollars. More shares at
lower prices generally benefit investors. Some astute professional investors, such as William Miller, will even assert that the person who gets the
lowest average price per share usually wins. Buying when prices are falling is typically a reliable way to reduce one's average price per share,
which sometimes magnifies future investment gains whenever share
prices recover.

To make sure you understand how this very important investment
concept works, let's look at one more example from a slightly different
perspective. Imagine that you allow yourself $100 a month to purchase
clothes. In January you buy a beautiful cashmere sweater for $100.
When February comes, you notice something very unusual at the department store. Cashmere sweaters are selling for only $5. It is February,
it is cold outside, you adore cashmere, and so you decide to spend the
whole $100 on new sweaters. You buy 20 more. You can't ever recall
such expensive sweaters selling for so little. March arrives and it is the
very same story. So, you buy 20 more sweaters. You now have 41 cashmere sweaters at a total cost of $300.

April rolls around and you discover that it is really an inconvenience
to have a closet full of 41 cashmere sweaters. You therefore organize a
neighborhood yard sale. You put these beautiful sweaters up for sale at
$25 a piece. Much to your surprise, 40 sweaters sell very quickly and you
rake in an easy $1,000. You not only more than tripled your money, but
you also were able to keep your favorite sweater from the lot. Basically,
that is what happens when you buy mutual fund shares at low prices.

Those who regularly defer money into a 401(k) plan each pay period
essentially follow the exact same strategy of the eager volunteer. Investors who stay the course and continue buying shares in their 401(k) plan
at work when prices are falling will likely experience the same fundamental results as the eager volunteer. This key feature of 401(k) plans—
investing uniform amounts of money each pay period—provides a way
for ordinary investors to successfully emulate smart money strategies
when prices are falling. Remember, 401(k) plans will automatically purchase shares at lower prices in soft markets, unless participants inter-

vene and either quit saving or direct the monies to cash. The basic 401(k) plan structure, however, is designed to give ordinary investors an advantage in the markets by adhering to a dollar-cost-averaging strategy. (Dollar cost averaging is nothing more than terminology describing the process of investing uniform amounts of money each pay period.) Keeping ordinary investors in the game when prices are falling is one of the most beneficial features of 401(k) plans. This vital design option gives ordinary people a tremendous edge as they save and invest for retirement.

Although the parameters in our hypothetical story are a bit exaggerated, a 95 percent decline in price is obviously extreme, such a story line is not altogether without historical precedent. For example, in September 1929, one month before the great stock market crash, the Dow Jones Industrial Average peaked at 381.17. Over the next 34 months, the Dow Jones Industrial Average fell nearly 90 percent, to 41.22. The stock market was 35 percent lower than where it stood at the end of 1899. The Dow, incidentally, did not fully recover in price until the decade of the 1950s. Those with the wisdom and fortitude and resources to keep buying shares in the Dow, however, could have theoretically broken even by 1934, or about two years after the market hit absolute bottom.

The purveyors of conventional wisdom often overlook this critically important dimension to making money. Falling prices in the stock market are almost always viewed with trepidation, whereas the news is often favorable for the savvy investor who is buying more shares. When oil prices drop, everyone, including those in the news media, rejoice—as they should. Lower gasoline prices mean most of us will have more money left over at the end of the month. Lower prices means dollars stretch further, whether one is buying gasoline, milk, diapers, or mutual fund shares. Lower prices, especially for those who are buyers, are almost always a positive.

When the prices of certain goods, such as soda pop, frozen dinners, or bananas, go on sale, stores will often place a limit on purchases. Limits are one way to prevent hoarding. *Hoarding* is basically what the eager volunteer did when his mutual fund shares plummeted to 0.50¢ a share in our story. He loaded up on as many shares as he could buy for $1,000 a month. The stock market, unlike conventional stores, will generally encourage investors to buy all the shares they can afford when stocks are on sale. Hoarding, on Wall Street, is a foreign concept. When stocks get cheap, buyers are scarce.

The road to wealth is full of ironies. The emotional pull of money sometimes creates a world that is upside down. Most people understand that when you buy a mutual fund and the price moves up, you make money. This is what conventional wisdom acknowledges. Most investors would readily admit it does feel good to look at a monthly statement and see an increase in one's account value as a result of higher prices. When stock prices go up, people get confident and want to pay more for fewer shares, whereas when the price of gasoline goes up, people grow fearful, get angry, and write Congress. Likewise, when stock prices go on sale, people have a tendency to panic and sell out, but when the price of gasoline drops, people celebrate and purchase new SUVs so they can buy more gas.

Smart money understands that lower prices are of great benefit to investors. Lower prices are like buying new cars below dealer invoice. The lower the price, the better, as long as you have the money to keep buying. This is the primary reason 401(k) retirement plans are such ingenious vehicles for the creation of personal wealth. Each month there is always more money to purchase more shares. And as we have just learned, the lower the prices, the more reasons smart money has to celebrate. Accumulating mutual fund shares at bargain-basement prices while others are in a panic and selling is immensely satisfying. Make sure when stocks are on sale, you and your financial professional are in agreement to get on the phone and touch base. Conditioning yourself to buy low, when saving for retirement, is one of the most significant aspects to successful saving.

The story of the eager volunteer is singular. It conveys one of the very few absolute rules of investing. Lower prices generally benefit buyers. Buy, therefore, when prices are low.

CHAPTER 13

Retirement Investments

It was the only time in his life that he relied solely on the expertise of
the Wall Street Journal, *or any information available on any street corner.*[1]
Jeffrey Archer, *Kane & Abel*

Hot Tips

More than 25 years ago British writer Jeffrey Archer published an enchanting novel about two young men, both of whom were extremely driven but from opposite ends of the socioeconomic ladder. These men, as one can probably already guess, end up as bitter rivals. Thus, the backdrop is set for what quickly unfolds as a breathtaking tale of money and power, jealousy and ambition, love and greed, and—eventually—resolution. It, like most of Archer's books, is a memorable page-turner.

Early on in this particular story there is an episode about one of the young men first starting out to invest in the stock market. He, like many investors new to the market, began buying stocks based on tips gleaned from the newspaper. Soon, however, the enterprising youngster had inadvertently lost nearly all of his money. He resolved, therefore, to never again rely on "any information available on any street corner."

Hot tips are omnipresent, meaning they are just everywhere. Often, when watching some business show on television, the anchor will press the on-air guest to give the viewers a couple of investment ideas. And sure enough, the on-air guest will offer two or three investment ideas or so-called hot tips. Just about anyone, with any interest in the stock market at all, will have an idea of something that is poised to move upward in price. Believe me, there is no shortage of stock tips.

The problem, unfortunately, is that hot tips seldom pan out—not because hot tips are necessarily bad tips, but rather because hot tips breed anxious money. A person who actually buys a security based on a hot tip generally has very urgent expectations for the stock or whatever is being purchased. When people put hard-earned money at risk in the markets, based on nothing more than someone's opinion, these people generally expect the stock or whatever to move up in price immediately. Should the stock or security purchased on a tip, however, languish or move down in price, those same people are likely to get impatient and sell, or panic and sell. Anxious money, as Jeffrey Archer so correctly intimated in his novel of 25 years ago, seldom multiplies.

Every great once in a while Warren Buffett will appear on television. Invariably, an interviewer will try to get Buffett to either make a market prediction or give a stock tip. Buffett adeptly dodges these questions. He has made it known for years that making short-term predictions on the market is completely foolish. No one, including Warren Buffett, can accurately predict what the market will do tomorrow or the next day or over the next year. It just can't be done. So, why in the world would any rational person ever attempt the impossible on television in front of millions of viewers? As for stock tips, Buffett, who is arguably the world's greatest investor, could really relay some interesting information in this regard. But, again, Buffett deftly refrains from engaging in such futility. A person with only a fraction of Buffett's intelligence can probably figure out that offering stock tips to the public as though it were "any information available on any street corner" could not possibly serve the interests of Buffett or his shareholders, and, curiously enough, even the general investing public, well. Experienced investors understand that emotion and stock tips are inseparable. Emotional money, as discussed earlier, is nothing more than anxious money. It has a miserable track record.

Hot tips shortcut the process of inversion. Tips, in other words, are a one-sided story. They paint the perfect picture of what could happen *if* all goes according to plan. Missing, unfortunately, is the rest of the story. That, in a sense, is what it means to "invert, always invert." Inversion leads one to the rest of the story. Inversion is what could happen when things don't necessarily follow the script. Does one sell everything when the bottom falls out? Does one buy more? People generally don't know what to do with hot tips when the story changes largely because they, as a rule, don't understand what it is they bought in the first place. It is the story of money getting invested for what often turns out to be insufficient cause.

It is quite possible that hot tips germinating around the water cooler have placed more retirement wealth in jeopardy than many of the broad-based market declines in recent history. The fear of getting left behind, while fellow co-workers are boasting about all the money being made by loading up on company stock or highly speculative mutual funds, has actually ruined workers financially in some cases. The great tales of tremendous financial achievement circulating around water coolers is usually just half of the story. The boring details such as lack of diversification, speculation, and reversion to the mean are often omitted from these heroic conversations.

Walk down any corridor in any company in any city and ask any employee about the investments in his or her 401(k) plan. The chances are good that people in many companies will not know what they own, how much they paid for it, how they would react to a nasty surprise in the market, or who they would call for professional advice. A person does not need to become an investment expert to retire wealthy, but as stated earlier, one does need a "willingness to understand and apply some basic ideas." Workers wishing to retire financially independent must be willing to take *ownership* of their saving and investing.

Balancing this, companies sponsoring 401(k) retirement plans should make certain their employees have full access to basic professional resources. Further, companies sponsoring 401(k) retirement programs should provide as much education as necessary to ensure that employees are never isolated and completely on their own when the critical tasks of saving sufficient sums and investing wisely are concerned. When there is a vacuum in the delivery of basic financial education and legitimate professional advice, retirement dreams and potential family fortunes are at great risk. Even though 401(k) plans are near-perfect instruments for the creation of personal retirement wealth, these retirement plans are not passive vehicles. Participants must learn what investments they should own and why, and who they can call when advice is necessary. Thoughtful education programs and professional advice, in short, offer workers the tools to ownership.

Retirement money is long-term money. Long-term money suppresses emotion and nervousness and urgency. Retirement money is rational money. It is invested thoughtfully. Retirement money is forward-looking money. The time horizon extends as far out as 20 and 30 years, perhaps even beyond. Retirement money is patient money. Forever is a very real possibility when working with retirement money. Hot, fast, and fleeting are foreign to retirement money. Long-term retirement money is grounded in reason, marked by confidence, and synonymous with fidelity.

Get Out of the Box

There are four stages of investing while becoming financially independent. The first two stages focus on increasing the value of your retirement assets on your personal balance sheet, and the final two stages concern generating enough income from your retirement assets to replace your job. Your balance sheet, as you may recall, is what defines your net worth. It balances what you own with what you owe. On one side are the assets; everything owned that could be converted to cash. Assets may include retirement monies, such as stocks, bonds, and mutual funds; home equity; gold coins; rental property; and whatever else you own that has monetary value. On the other side are your debts or liabilities. Liabilities include your home mortgage, outstanding car loans, student loans, credit card debt, and whatever else you might owe someone. Subtracting liabilities from your assets produces a number, which is your net worth. For our purposes, the most important item on this personal balance sheet is the value of your retirement assets. This is the number that will most likely determine your standard of living in retirement.

The first stage of wealth creation is what I like to call "getting out of the box." It is what Charlie Munger identifies as being the most difficult part of building wealth: going from zero net worth to $100,000. Until you surpass the $100,000 mark, you remain inside the box. The longer you remain inside the box, with retirement assets under $100,000, the less likely it becomes that you will achieve financial independence by retirement age. Workers must therefore try to do everything within their power to get out of the box as soon as possible.

Although investing plays an important role, the real key to getting out of the box, or achieving $100,000 as soon as possible, is saving sufficient sums. Because saving in the initial stage of getting out of the box is so very important, some may want to consider taking on additional part-time work, committing to working overtime, or putting off the purchase of all big-ticket items until the $100,000 mark is achieved. You will likely reach your first $100,000, not because investments performed brilliantly, but rather because you saved aggressively, if not sacrificially. Contrary to conventional thought, even superior investment results are unlikely to compensate for insufficient savings when it comes to achieving the first $100,000. Starting from zero savings, the average person will need to save around $68,000 to get out of the box within 10 years; to get out within 12 years, that person will need to save $63,000. The point is clear: Those who rely solely on spectacular investment results to get out of the box seldom make it.

During the introductory stage of wealth creation, the getting out of the box stage, workers have an opportunity to learn the basic fundamentals of investing wisely. And even though investment mistakes are undesirable, they are seldom fatal during this initial period. Saving sufficient sums, after all, is the train carrying most all the freight. For example, let's say an investor has $20,000 in his account and makes a mistake that causes his account to fall by 20 percent. The person will suffer a $4,000 loss. Although painful, suffering a 20 percent loss on $20,000 is inconsequential compared with a 20 percent loss on $200,000. Now we're talking about a loss of $40,000, or one year's pay for the average American worker. That is the one beauty of being in the box. Investors have a real opportunity to learn "hands-on investing" without suffering serious consequences. The investment knowledge acquired during these early years can prove invaluable once one passes the $100,000 mark and investing takes on additional relevance.

There are five guiding principles participants need to know as they make their investments. First, they need to know what it is they own. Second, investors need to know why they own it. Third, people should know precisely what action they plan to take in the event of a market panic. Fourth, workers must know how to respond whenever a fellow employee brags at the water cooler about an investment that was up 45 percent last week and is poised to go to the moon. And finally, investors need to know who to call for professional investment advice. These five fundamentals are all basic, but they will make a critical difference in a worker's investment results.

Those adhering to these five principles will eventually develop a personal investment philosophy. Such a fundamental approach encourages 401(k) participants to use reason over emotion when selecting investments. Further, nervous speculation is suppressed in favor of a seasoned long-term perspective. The emphasis on investing moves away from day-to-day fluctuations in price to the ultimate financial goal of individual wealth at retirement.

Five Guiding Principles of 401(k) Investing

1. Know what you own
2. Know why you own it
3. Know what to do in a panic
4. Know how to handle water-cooler hyperbole
5. Know who to call for professional advice

There are any number of investment choices that will serve investors well during the introductory stage of wealth creation. There are so many choices, in fact, that the selection process can become overwhelming. After adding all the different investment options available to American investors, the gross number easily surpasses 25,000 different vehicles. There are mutual funds, annuity products, exchange-traded funds, hedge funds, real estate investment trusts, limited partnerships, closed-end mutual funds, separately managed accounts, certificates of deposit, individual stocks, corporate bonds, government bonds, agency bonds, as well as money market funds. When it comes to investment choice, this is the country! Believe what you will about Wall Street, but when it comes to the packaging and promotion of money, nobody manufactures more.

For those who invest in 401(k)s, the trustees to your plan have done much of the initial screening already. Most plans offer anywhere from 5 to 50 different choices. Generally speaking, the vast majority of 401(k) plans will offer mutual funds as the primary investment vehicle. Further, participants often receive favorable pricing on mutual fund shares when purchased inside a 401(k) plan. Larger corporations may also offer the opportunity to purchase company stock in their own 401(k) plans. It is

then typically the employee's responsibility to take the universe of options available in his or her 401(k) and build a retirement portfolio.

It is my firm belief that investors who are in the introductory stage
of investing, meaning retirement assets are below $100,000, should own
mutual funds that invest primarily in common stocks. Unless one owns
common stocks, it is going to be very difficult to achieve normal investment returns. Depending on one's age and other considerations, one's
investment professional may wish to have that person also invest in
bonds. Holding some cash or some bonds is perfectly acceptable, but,
when your total retirement assets are below $100,000, it makes sense to
accumulate as many mutual fund shares as possible that are invested in
common stocks.

To understand better the investment selection process for a 401(k),
let's explore a hypothetical situation. Imagine that you are a relatively new
participant in a 401(k) plan. Your investment advisor recommends that
you put 100 percent of your account balance into a large cap equity mutual fund. The professional also has advised you to allocate 100 percent
of your weekly deferrals into this same large cap stock fund.

Know What You Own

A large cap mutual fund is a specific type of investment comprised
of very large public corporations. Usually a company will need to have a
market valuation or capitalization (hence the abbreviation, cap) of at
least $10 billion. There will be at least 50 to 100 stocks in this mutual
fund. You will recognize most of the names. Companies in the fund
could include such well-known names as Coca-Cola, Wal-Mart, General
Electric, Microsoft, or Pfizer. Large cap funds, as a rule, invest in big,
blue-chip companies. A team of portfolio managers employed by the
mutual fund makes the investment decisions. This means the names of
companies in the mutual fund will change from time to time. For example, if the managers think a recession is on the horizon, they may sell a
stock such as Caterpillar and replace it with a more recession-proof company such as Colgate-Palmolive. Finally, because these are large, well-
established companies, many of them will pay dividends. These dividends
could have an average annual return of 2 percent.

Know Why You Own It

There are several reasons an investor might want to own a well-diversified, large cap mutual fund. First, and perhaps most importantly, it is very unlikely that such a fund would ever go to zero and become worthless. Like all stock investments, the prices on mutual funds will fluctuate daily. The prices on this type of fund may very well fall below your purchase price, meaning that if you sell shares below the price paid, you will lose money. There is absolutely no guarantee that you will make money on this type of investment. Although the prices on the investment will fluctuate up and down, it is nonetheless highly unlikely that investors will lose everything. This, as we learned earlier, provides a very important reason for owning the fund. It will allow you to justify buying more shares whenever prices do fall in value. Lower prices mean investors get more shares for their money.

A large cap mutual fund is the type of investment that a person could own forever. While individual stocks can sometimes get into trouble, owning 50 to 100 of America's largest companies (wherein a professional portfolio manager or team of managers is watching over the stocks) is the type of investment that could endure for several lifetimes. Many mutual funds today were actually started in the 1920s and 1930s. Sometime within the next 25 years, there will be mutual funds celebrating centennial anniversaries.

A third reason for owning a large cap mutual fund is the investment performance, which should achieve normal returns over long-term time horizons of 20 to 30 years. An important objective when owning a large cap stock mutual fund over long periods of time is to outperform bonds and cash. As long as the American economy continues to innovate and grow, large cap funds should produce quite satisfactory returns over time. These funds are in many ways a proxy for the American economy.

Know What to Do in a Panic

When a panic erupts, investors who own large cap mutual funds should plan to buy more shares at lower prices. This is the primary reason behind knowing what one owns. When people know their investments as well as farmers understand farmland, they are able to buy more when prices are collapsing. Panics scare away those who do not understand what it is they own. *Investors should never, ever put a cent into any investment they would not want more of when prices get cheaper.* Money is made in market downturns by taking definitive action and buying more shares. Panics create lower prices that, in turn, offer investors wonderful opportunities to make money by buying low and then selling at higher prices.

Know How to Handle Water-Cooler Hyperbole

What do you say to the person at the water cooler who is bragging about being up 45 percent in his or her latest investment? Well, first offer congratulations. That is very impressive performance. Second, be careful about jumping to conclusions. Sometimes the immediate response for people upon hearing this news is to go out and jump on the bandwagon. Remember, however, that anyone who now buys this same security is paying a 45 percent premium just to get on board. It is the same thing as someone coming to work and saying, "Boy, I just bought this great television set for $250." Then when you run out to buy the very same television the price is now $350. (Which represents a 40 percent premium.) Would you still jump to buy the exact same television? Most people would probably want to take some extra time and think through the implications of paying such a high premium for the exact same set.

Thoughtlessly jumping on bandwagons is a serious mistake made by many investors. It is called *extrapolation*. People have a tendency to extrapolate performance from the past and project it to the future. For example, when someone says his or her investment is up by 45 percent, our response is to sometimes think the investment will keep going up by that same amount. It is a common error.

Know what you own and why you own it. Then, if you really want to explore the great idea at the water cooler, call your investment professional. Maybe the investment that was up 45 percent still possesses promising long-term potential. That is one reason to work closely with a financial professional. Just remember, unless you already own the investment with those great numbers, that really great past performance always belongs to someone else.

Know Who to Call for Professional Advice

A professional is someone who has experience performing difficult tasks over and over and over again until he or she is able to get it right nearly every time. People will go through the process of building retirement wealth only once in their lifetimes. Mistakes are costly because there often is not time enough to correct serious errors. The role professional advice plays is extremely important when it comes to personal retirement planning because lost time is so unforgiving. Many can competently travel the road to retirement alone, but most employees will benefit from a helping hand. Great retirement plans offer participants wise professional counsel. Make sure you get to know a professional you can trust and call upon throughout this journey.

The five guiding principles of 401(k) investing have a very simple purpose: to wring the emotion and nervousness out of retirement money. Before you put money into any investment, make sure you adhere to these basic principles. Never take anything for granted. Take the time to know what you own, why you own it, and always have a prepared plan for panic. You also do not have to load the boat with a lot of different mutual funds. Remember, these investments are widely diversified. Some funds may even own hundreds of different stocks or bonds. You don't need 5,000 stocks or bonds to get wealthy! Two or three funds investing in a total of several hundred different securities capable of generating normal investment returns will serve you very well, especially if you buy like crazy when others are heading for the exits. Mastering these five guiding principles when in the box will prepare you well for the second stage of becoming financially independent.

Marlboro Friday

Jeremy Siegel is a leading expert on the stock market. A professor at the Wharton School of Business, he has written two excellent books on stocks and the market. In his most recent book, *The Future for Investors,* Siegel makes the interesting observation that "reinvesting dividends is the critical factor giving the edge to most winning stocks in the long run."[2] To illustrate his point, he writes about Philip Morris stock and an event called "Marlboro Friday." His work on Marlboro Friday brought to mind a true story that happened to me on that very same weekend.

"I heard you might know something about 401(k) plans." This is how a neighbor first introduced himself to me one Sunday in 1993. On Friday, April 2, Philip Morris stock (since renamed Altria) tumbled by 23 percent in a single day. The sudden collapse caught both the stock market and certainly Philip Morris shareholders completely by surprise. This fateful day is still remembered vividly by many as Marlboro Friday.

The person who found his way to me worked for a local subsidiary of Philip Morris. He owned Philip Morris stock in his company 401(k) plan. Incredibly, if I recall correctly, it could have been the only thing he owned in his 401(k) plan. When he went to work on Friday morning, his 401(k) account was worth around $500,000. On the way home that evening, his 401(k) was down to $400,000. His account had dropped in value by approximately $100,000 within a single day. The man appeared devastated. The hardest part of building wealth, getting to $100,000 from a net worth of zero, was stripped away from this participant in minutes. The man explained that he had hoped to retire within five years. He was now uncertain as to whether this would ever happen. Someone told him I might be able to help.

There are two very important lessons investors must learn when they are in the box, meaning their retirement assets are under $100,000. They must first learn to save aggressively. That means they should be prepared to save 20 percent of their annual income. The second lesson they must master is the five guiding principles of 401(k) investing. It is very, very difficult to become financially independent until one attains $100,000 in retirement assets and then learns how to invest this money.

The neighbor I met on Marlboro Friday weekend had obviously mastered the first lesson, which is the most difficult part of building wealth, but he unfortunately still had some work to do on the second lesson concerning the five guiding principles of 401(k) investing. This second lesson is becoming more and more significant as many corporations are now terminating traditional defined benefit pension plans and setting up 401(k) plans. Responsibility for handling the retirement investments is falling upon the shoulders of workers. It is of paramount importance for workers to now know how one must invest in a 401(k).

Applying the five guiding principles of 401(k) investing to the neighbor's personal circumstances might help the reader better understand how these simple principles work in the real world. First, the neighbor no doubt understood what he was buying. He was an employee of a major Philip Morris subsidiary. It is probably safe to assume that he was aware of the major business units, each unit's contributions to annual revenues, as well as earning projections. The man had not flippantly just thrown a half million dollars into a company of which he had no knowledge. Second, the neighbor also knew why he owned the stock. Philip Morris delivered strong investment performance. The neighbor believed that Philip Morris could deliver better investment performance than the other mutual fund alternatives in his 401(k) plan. So, the man knew what he owned and he knew why he owned it. He did not, however, have a plan for panic. When the stock plummeted unexpectedly, he was not sure what to do next. Remember, hardly anyone will see a panic coming. Getting surprised is not the issue. Everyone, sooner or later, gets surprised. The critical issue is, What does one do after the initial shock? The answer is to buy more. If you cannot bring yourself to buy more after a panic, then you own the wrong investment. The neighbor loaded the boat with Philip Morris stock because he was most likely chasing performance, not because he believed the stock could ever get hammered. When his performance and $100,000 vanished within minutes, there was no longer any reason to own the stock. This is one way panics and massive sell-offs in the markets get acerbated.

The neighbor was also not very good at managing water-cooler hyperbole. Again, I am reasonably sure he was not the only one who left work on Friday a lot poorer. Usually when things like this happen, there are all kinds of people throughout the company who make the very same mistake. Water-cooler talk is not isolated. When things are going great, there is nothing better than having all your eggs in one basket. On the other hand, when that one basket hits the floor, there is nothing like diversification. A great many employees learned a very valuable lesson on the importance of owning 401(k) investments that are spread out among scores of different securities on that Friday. That is a key reason mutual funds are such appropriate investment vehicles for 401(k) plans. Mutual funds are diversified investments. Finally, the neighbor obviously did not know who to call in the midst of this panic. Introducing oneself to a complete stranger with the flattering words "I *heard* you *might* know something about 401(k) plans" has got to be a painful line to deliver.

Fortunately, this man's circumstances were not as dire as they appeared. When the stock plummeted, he did not sell his shares into the panic. He remained with his investment in Philip Morris. Second, he sought advice. I am sure that he consulted with others in addition to me before making any changes in his 401(k). And third, his portfolio was structured to survive a market downturn better than many 401(k) accounts with significant market values greater than $100,000. His portfolio produced income, in fact, lots of income.

The second stage of achieving financial independence occurs when one's retirement assets surpass $100,000. The second stage will take investors from $100,000 to their retirement goal. The key thing one must always prepare for in this second stage is a severe market drop. Workers don't want to go from $500,000 to $250,000 or even $400,000 for that matter. One way to protect these assets is to make sure one's retirement investments are properly diversified and generate substantial amounts of income. Income is derived from either dividends or bond interest.

For illustrative purposes, let's assume the neighbor owned 8,000 shares of Philip Morris stock. On April 1, the stock closed at $64.12. The stock, incidentally, was paying annual dividends to shareholders of $2.60 a share at that time. This means the neighbor with 8,000 shares was receiving approximately $20,800 each year in dividend income. On April 2, the stock closed at $49.38 a share. The stock was still paying, however, $2.60 in dividends. This meant that the neighbor, by continuing to hold Philip Morris stock, could purchase $20,800 worth of additional stock each year at bargain-basement prices. It was rather obvious that as long as Philip Morris continued to pay the dividend, the neighbor could dig his way out by reinvesting the dividends into more Philip Morris shares. To begin diversifying his portfolio, he could start taking his payroll savings and buy mutual fund shares. With the income from his Philip Morris shares, he could buy more stock at the lower prices.

To make sure you understand the importance of income in a portfolio, let's review once more the preceding strategy. There are three possible sources of income in your 401(k) account. First, there are salary deferrals. This is the money you save from your paycheck. Second, there are contributions that could come from your company. These monies are paid as matching contributions or company profit-sharing contributions. (Please understand that not all companies, however, make matching or profit-sharing contributions.) Third, there is income generated from investments if you select securities that pay dividends or bond interest. Once you pass the $100,000 mark, it is always a good idea to own securities that produce income. In this example, the neighbor owned Philip Morris stock that generated more than $20,000 a year in new income.

Because the neighbor had most of his eggs in one basket, he needed to diversify away from having most of his money in Philip Morris stock. He could easily do this by taking the income from his salary deferrals and any company contributions, if applicable, and purchase mutual fund shares. The second part to the strategy concerned Philip Morris stock. Here he could have taken the rich dividends and continued to purchase more shares of Philip Morris at steeply discounted prices. Scooping up all these shares when the stock price was cheap would help him accelerate the recovery of his money whenever Philip Morris rebounded.

It took almost two years for Philip Morris stock to recover fully from Marlboro Friday. During that interval, the company not only paid eight quarterly dividends, but it raised the dividend payment two times. If the neighbor reinvested all of these dividends into Philip Morris stock, his holdings would have been worth $570,000 within two years. Now that he was safely out of the hole, he could diversify his Philip Morris holdings among several mutual fund selections. Additionally, he would also have accumulated 2 years of mutual fund shares through his salary deferrals. It was almost as though nothing ever happened.[3]

Jeremy Siegel, in *The Future for Investors,* underscores "two important ways that dividends will help investors in bear markets."[4] First, dividends will cushion a decline in stocks whenever the income is used to purchase additional shares at lower prices. He calls the repurchase of shares at bargain-basement prices the "bear market protector."[5] Second, once share prices recover fully, the reinvestment of dividends turns into what he calls a "return accelerator."[6] We were able to see both of these dynamics in the example concerning my former neighbor. "This is why," according to Siegel, "dividend paying stocks provide the highest return over stock market cycles."[7] That, in a nutshell, is the surprising outcome of Marlboro Friday.

The lessons you learn through the different stages of wealth accumulation are cumulative. You will continue to practice what you gained knowledge of throughout your investing lifetime. Save 20 percent of your income. Master the five guiding principles of 401(k) investing. And once you pass the $100,000 mark, make sure you and your financial professional construct a retirement portfolio to include investments that produce income and are well diversified. Even though 20 percent market or investment declines are rare events, they do sometimes happen. Portfolios that generate meaningful income give you money, in addition to your salary deferrals, that can purchase more shares at lower prices should your investments drop significantly. Always own securities that you want to buy more of, and always allocate resources so that you'll have the income to make those purchases.

CHAPTER 14

Managing Your Retirement Portfolio

It won't be the American economy, in my view, that does in investors over a 5-, 10-, or 20-year period–it will be investors themselves.[1]
Warren Buffett

Over Thinking Can Cost You a Lot of Money

There are worse things in life than watching others get wealthy faster than you. Suffering anxiety over watching someone make what is believed to be a lot of money can cause people to fall into the trap of over thinking. For example, the business section to a national paper recently carried an article in which a couple of well-known investment managers thought one particular group of stocks would likely outperform another group of stocks over the next year or two. These types of articles are fodder for over thinkers. Over thinkers who read them immediately start worrying about their retirement portfolios, especially if they own some of the stocks in question. Those who over think always seem to second guess themselves and thus produce a surfeit of needless problems.

Years ago I asked an executive of the firm where I was working to prepare a special report for me. This particular firm sponsored a terrific retirement plan in which every year the company gave all the eligible employees a contribution that equaled 15 percent of their annual wages. I was curious as to how many millionaires were in the company retirement plan, so I asked this person to prepare a study comprised of just one number. No names, just the number. When the executive returned with the report, the number was truly amazing. Basically, if I recall correctly, almost 1 out of 20 eligible participants had an account balance in excess of $1 million. (This incidentally was several years before the stock market reached all-time highs in 2000.) Also, higher-paid executives were capped at contributions that were far less than 15 percent of their wages due to IRS regulations. The results of this informal study seemed exceedingly clear. There were a lot of long-time workers at the company with a substantial net worth as a result of the firm's generous retirement plan. Putting away 15 percent of one's wages, year after year, regardless of whether the money comes from one's company or one's paycheck, is likely to accumulate into substantial sums over time when that money gets invested wisely.

Interestingly, the investment choices available to employees at the time were somewhat limited. The program did not offer 40, 50, or 60 different choices. Most of the money could have been found in three or four core mutual funds. None of the mutual funds were too fancy or sophisticated. There was a highly regarded large cap fund, an excellent corporate bond fund, and some smaller funds. The investment selections were comprised of very basic offerings. It was not the type of investment menu that lent itself to a lot of over thinking by over thinkers.

It is a myth, in my judgment, to think you have to own a whole bunch of investments in your portfolio to accumulate meaningful wealth over a working lifetime. A good stock fund and an excellent corporate bond fund ought to get the job done just fine. This type of approach has worked well for many who now are comfortably retired, and it should also work well for you. Do not be afraid of simplicity. Simplicity is your friend; simplicity will serve you well on the road to wealth. Invest in something, such as high-quality mutual funds, that can last forever. Then, as covered earlier, make sure you understand what you own, why you own it, and be prepared to buy more when others are panicking and the prices are cheap. Believe me, you don't need 40 investment alternatives to execute such a strategy. You also don't need to keep switching your investments all the time. Beware of those who would try to lure you away from a credible long-term investment by promoting some other security with better performance numbers during the past three or five years. Making frequent changes among funds is often indicative of poor judgment. It is one more symptom of anxious money. Anxiety about getting left behind the rest of the pack should not concern you as long as you have money going into respectable funds year after year.

Not all funds are obviously equal. The inequality among investment choices becomes particularly relevant once an investor crosses the $100,000 mark in retirement savings. Once you've arrived at that point where your investments need to be pulling your wealth forward, it is important to identify some real workhorses for the rest of the journey. The investment mix or asset allocation of your portfolio is critical at this important juncture.

I have always been particularly partial to large capitalization stocks. If I were to purchase an index fund, I would favor the S&P 500. It is comprised, as we discussed earlier, of 500 of the largest companies in the United States. This type of index fund is easy to understand, extremely well diversified, and an excellent choice for buying more when prices are falling. Additionally, and this is very important, the S&P 500 pays a dividend. Income, as we learned in the story of Marlboro Friday, is very important once one crosses the $100,000 mark. Finally, index funds generally have very low annual fees. Owning a piece of 500 of the largest companies in America through an index fund is an investment that fits my understanding of holding something forever.

Many readers may not have access to an S&P 500 fund in their 401(k) plan. Instead, you will likely have other mutual funds, some of which will be comprised of large capitalization stocks. Many of these large cap mutual funds have been around for 50 years or longer. Key here, at least in my judgment, is to select a large cap fund that serves as one of the flagship funds for a particular mutual fund family. Most mutual fund complexes will offer a wide variety of funds. Those funds that have been around for some time and have an abundance of the total assets under management in a particular fund complex often carry certain advantages. For example, let's imagine that a particular fund complex has a total of $100 billion under management. The $100 billion is spread among 20 different funds; $40 billion, however, is in the firm's large cap mutual fund, which means 40 percent of the fund complex's assets are in one single mutual fund. From a business perspective, it is rather clear that the executives at this particular investment company are going to watch the mutual fund with $40 billion very closely. The reputation of the entire investment company firm, after all, is mostly riding on this one fund with $40 billion. Therefore, the portfolio manager or team of managers running the investments on that flagship fund are likely to be very experienced and talented. It is unlikely, in other words, that a fund complex will hire a kid fresh out of college and let him "cut his teeth" on the firm's flagship fund. It is in everyone's best interest for flagship funds to do well. Sometimes, reviewing all the mutual funds available in a 401(k) is a very confusing process. If you are completely unfamiliar with a particular mutual fund complex or the investments offered, a good place to start is by finding the so-called flagship funds. These flagship funds may not always be the very top performers, but at least you'll know the people running them are competent.

A person may experience an additional sense of security whenever he or she is familiar with the investments in a particular mutual fund. That is one major reason I have always favored large company stocks. I know something firsthand about many bellwether stocks. Names such as General Electric, Microsoft, and Coca-Cola are not foreign to me. The products made by these firms play an active role in my daily life. Having a basic idea of just what exactly a particular mutual fund owns is important. It helps to visualize holdings. These types of stocks match my personality well. They provide serenity.

You must understand, however, that not everyone is enamored with such a simplistic approach to investing. There are many who will argue that large flagship funds are not able to perform as well as smaller funds that are believed to be more nimble. While such an argument may be true in some instances, it is not a universal truth. There are many large flagship funds that consistently perform well. Selecting flagship funds is a sound investment strategy.

Next, you must be aware that others are convinced that investing in small, individual company stocks will produce better returns over time than large-company stocks. The thinking here is that smaller companies are able to grow earnings faster than large companies. Companies with faster earnings growth will typically produce higher stock prices. There is indeed merit to such thinking. Investing in smaller-company stocks does have many advantages, especially when one is investing for long time periods of 20 to 30 years. Those who feel very strongly about the investment attributes of small-company stocks may want to add a small cap mutual fund to their retirement portfolio. Investors with an independent interest in these types of securities must make sure, however, that they understand that prices on small companies can be a bit more volatile than large companies, and be prepared to do additional homework.

It also is important to mention international or foreign stocks. As economies across the globe continue to expand, America's portion of the total world pie continues to shrink, while other countries gain a larger slice. There are many who therefore advocate the ownership of foreign securities that can hopefully capitalize on this international growth trend. International markets do, however, subject investors to new types of risk. Many countries have different financial accounting standards, varied geopolitical structures, less liquid and regulated stock markets, and sometimes volatile currency exchange rates. Meanwhile, there are many large U.S. corporations that are multinational entities already participating in these vibrant and emerging economies. Investors, by owning large, multinational U.S. firms that are found in large cap flagship mutual funds, can easily gain international exposure without actually owning foreign shares. This is not to suggest that large U.S. entities are the perfect substitute for investing overseas in an international mutual fund. Nonetheless, should a panic situation ever erupt in some overseas market, the typical investor is more likely to put more money into large U.S. company stocks that are on sale than in a foreign market in which it is difficult to understand the underlying dynamics. Again, it basically boils down to the five guiding principles of 401(k) investing. Investing some portion of your retirement assets in foreign markets is an acceptable strategy as long as you understand what you own, why you own it, and are able to buy more shares in a market downturn. Those who are uncertain as to whether they will be able to respond boldly should foreign markets ever get cheaper can still profit from overseas economic growth by investing in large multinational companies domiciled at home.

One must remember that the objective of investing is to accomplish important financial goals in life. Owning large flagship funds for 20, 30, or 40 years with top-notch investment management teams that invest primarily in large cap companies is one practical approach to achieving normal investment results. Such a strategy does not require one to over think the investment process. Owning large flagship funds is not the only approach to producing normal investment returns nor will it necessarily always produce the very best investment results, but this style of investing is easy for the average person to comprehend and easy to implement. What negligible returns might be lost in performance are often offset by a good night's sleep.

The Importance of Fixed Income

Once a person surpasses $100,000 in retirement assets, there are several new challenges that confront the individual investor. First, one must continue to save aggressively and invest wisely to accumulate enough wealth by retirement age to replace one's job. Moving from $100,000 to one's final retirement goal is the second stage of the journey to financial independence. It is critical to keep building impressive retirement wealth during this second stage. Second, one must be careful not to suffer terrific losses along the way. As mentioned earlier, a 20 percent loss on $200,000 is the equivalent of the average family's annual wages in America. Market downturns can usually be softened by adding income-producing vehicles to one's retirement portfolio. Bonds, which are known as fixed-income securities, generate cash for purchasing additional shares, especially in the event of a market downturn. Additionally, bonds diversify the securities in one's portfolio. It is for these reasons fixed income or bonds play an important role in a person's investment strategy once the $100,000 threshold is passed: Bonds decrease volatility in a portfolio, diversify investment assets, and produce cash for the purchase of additional shares.

Most 401(k) plans offer participants the option of investing in a mutual fund consisting of corporate bonds. Typically, corporate bond funds will pay a higher rate of interest than government bonds because corporate bonds are going to be perceived as being a bit riskier than securities backed by the full faith and credit of the U.S. government. To compensate for this risk, corporate bond funds are usually very well diversified. Some funds will hold anywhere from 300 to 1,000 different bonds. The portfolio managers will own a great variety of different maturities, meaning some bonds will mature in a year or two while others may extend maturities out as far as 30 years and even beyond. Because corporate bond funds generally own hundreds of different bonds, the fund will hold several types of fixed-income securities that could include government bonds, government agency bonds, convertible bonds, high-grade corporates, as well as high-yield or junk bonds.

Corporate bond funds are considered to be less volatile than stock or equity mutual funds. This means prices typically do not fluctuate up and down as much in a bond fund as in a stock fund. As a general rule, whenever stocks are charging upward in price, bond prices will typically lag behind. Conversely, whenever stock prices are spiraling downward, bond prices will often hold steady. Again, these are broad generalities that may or may not hold true depending on specific circumstances. Like a stock fund, bond funds are not guaranteed investments. Prices will fluctuate daily. If you sell at a price lower than your purchase price, you will lose money when investing in a bond fund. Bond prices move in the opposite direction of interest rates. For instance, when interest rates fall, bond prices go up; when interest rates rise, bond prices fall.

Asset Allocation

Discovering the proper balance between stocks and bonds in a portfolio is one of the most difficult tasks of investing. This process is called *asset allocation*. Asset allocation is the science of distributing different investments within a portfolio. For example, how much of a person's portfolio should be dedicated to stocks, and what percentage should be assigned to bonds? There are many important factors to consider when contemplating these questions. There have been periods in American history when stocks were considered too risky for retirement accounts. Having 100 percent of one's retirement money in fixed-income vehicles made perfect sense for some financial experts even before, and certainly after, the crash of 1929. It took a long time for many investors to recover psychologically from the great crash. Stocks were synonymous with speculation and gambling. In Germany, however, the hyperinflation of the 1920s had just the opposite effect on investment sentiment. There, it was bondholders who got wiped out. Whenever housewives are pushing wheelbarrows full of money to the grocery, it is obvious that bonds are on the way to oblivion. As you can see, investor sentiment and psychology play prominent roles in asset allocation.

From an individual perspective, the considerations surrounding asset allocation are a bit more personal. Those who are perceived as aggressive investors will sometimes want to be over weighted in stocks. For example, there are many who are completely comfortable owning nothing but stocks in their retirement portfolios. Younger workers may shun fixed income while older investors sometimes prefer nothing but bonds and certificates of deposit. Those with little time left to work and save are often leery of losing money in the stock market. Individual perspective, therefore, gives considerable weight to factors such as personal investment style and age when determining the allocation of assets between stocks and bonds.

When investing for financial independence, it is my opinion that the primary determinant concerning asset allocation is the relationship between your ultimate retirement goal and the progress you are making toward achieving that goal. The current balance of your retirement account, in other words, and its relationship to your financial goal at retirement, is the key factor when determining asset allocation. Investment sentiment and psychology, age, and investment style are all important considerations, but it is your tangible progress in building wealth over time, or *dollar amount saved in relation to your goal dollar amount,* that should determine the formula for your asset allocation. Changing the mix between bonds and stocks (asset allocation) plays a strategic function in your portfolio. Stocks fuel growth, whereas bonds temper volatility and generate cash for the purpose of purchasing more stock. The mixture between stocks and bonds should change as your retirement assets grow. The more your retirement assets multiply, the more bonds you'll want to own. Now, because it takes the majority of a working lifetime to become wealthy, you'll also own more bonds as you grow older. So, as your retirement assets increase and your age increases, so too will the number of bonds you own increase as well. The key determinant, however, is not so much age as it is the progress being made in the accumulation of your money as it relates to your goal.

The formula for asset allocation works as follows: If an investor's account balance represents 20 percent of the retirement goal, then that person should have 20 percent of his or her assets in bonds and 80 percent in stocks. If an investor's account balance represents 50 percent of the retirement goal, then that person should have 50 percent in bonds and 50 percent in stock. The formula works all the way up the ladder until the investor reaches 84 percent of the retirement goal. Once one has achieved 84 percent of his or her goal, with 84 percent of those assets in bonds, he or she does not need to add any more bonds to the mix. The investor will complete the remainder of the retirement goal with stocks. At retirement, that person will want to have 70 percent of his or her portfolio in bonds (retirement income) and 30 percent in stocks (protection against inflation).

Let's take a look at some examples. A person has a retirement goal of $1,000,000 and an account balance of $150,000. Because $150,000 represents 15 percent of $1,000,000, or 15 percent of the given retirement goal, that investor would want to have $22,500, or 15 percent of his or her account balance, in bonds and $127,500 in stocks (15 percent of $150,000 = $22,500; 85 percent of $150,000 = $127,500).

Let's examine one more illustration. An investor has a retirement goal of $800,000 and an account balance of $256,000. The account balance represents 32 percent of his or her retirement goal ($256,000 ÷ $800,000 = 32 percent). That investor would want to have approximately $82,000 in bonds ($256,000 × 0.32 = $81,920) and $174,000 in stocks (0.68 × $256,000 = $174,080).

Bonds may not necessarily make you rich, but they can help keep you from becoming poor. Once you cross the $100,000 mark, you're dealing with serious money. Because your money is now working for you in a meaningful way, the second $100,000 should come much more easily than the first $100,000 dollars. As your wealth grows from $100,000 to $200,000 to $300,000 to $400,000, you surely do not want to suffer steep losses and thus get into a situation wherein you must retrace steps. Bonds are intended to diversify wealth, soften downturns, and provide ready cash for the continual accumulation of additional shares.

Bond Allocation Formula

Step 1: Divide value of retirement account by retirement goal.

Step 2: Multiply result of Step 1 by your retirement account value.

Example: A person's account value is $150,000. The retirement goal is $1,000,000.

Step 1: $150,000 ÷ $1,000,000 = 0.15

Step 2: $150,000 × 0.15 = $22,500

$22,500 should be allocated to bonds.

Buying Bonds

The long-term approach to wealth creation, which can take 30 to 40 years, exposes individual investors to numerous advantages. For example, when one is building wealth over such an extended time period, that person will have the luxury of exercising patience. There is never a rush to buy anything. An investor can determine a fair price and then wait for the market to come around with the desired offer. Urgency is the master of speculation, whereas investment basks in the luxury of patience.

Bonds are described as being *fixed*-income investments, which means the interest rate is fixed by the price of the bond. If a bond pays a fixed rate of 3 percent, then that is the return on your money you should expect to receive. Bond funds, unlike bonds, do not have maturity dates, so the fixed rate for the fund will change, but the general principle still basically holds true. You will want to buy bonds or bond funds when the rate of return is high and the price is low. Bonds are interest rate sensitive, meaning their prices are largely determined by the level at which interest rates are trading. High interest rates are music to the ears of long-term bond buyers. Because you are going to put the income from your bond fund to work, you will want the return to be as high as is reasonably feasible.

A good corporate bond fund, as described earlier, is well diversified among several types of bonds. These funds will generally have higher returns than government bond funds and lower returns than high-yield or junk bond funds. Because the new money you put into a corporate bond fund will be long-term money, there is no reason to chase yield. There is plenty of time to exercise patience. For example, if a very reputable corporate bond fund is paying 5 percent, but someone else is promoting a product showing 10 percent, be careful. There are all kinds of ways to artificially inflate rates. Excess fixed-income returns generally come with excessive risks. As a rule of thumb, it is usually best to stay with quality and wait for the market to come to you.

Interest rate cycles have a tendency to be rather long term. That means if interest rates are low, they will often remain low for years and years. Conversely, when interest rates are high, they will likely stay elevated for years. Within these cycles, however, there are sometimes terrific opportunities for the patient investor. It really boils down to knowing where to look for what it is you want.

Several years ago there was an interview in *Barrons,* a weekly financial newspaper published by Dow Jones.[2] Joe Rosenberg, a long-time professional investor, was making some observations on the stock market. It was April 1997 and stocks were on the way to the moon. From 1982 through 1997, the stock market had been compounding at an unbelievably high rate of 18.5 percent a year. Everyone wanted to own stocks. And most everyone who owned stocks was making tons of money. To put this in perspective for you, if someone had invested $100,000 in stocks around 1982, by 1997 that money (including dividends) would have been worth more than $1.2 million. It was in the midst of this tremendous bull market that a reporter asked Joe Rosenberg to offer his opinion on the stock market. Rosenberg, drawing from more than 30 years of experience, responded by saying there is no way the stock market can continue to go up by 18.5 percent a year forever. The party is going to someday end. But, continued Rosenberg, there is something that can go on for the next 20 to 25 years at the wonderful rate of around 7 percent. It is government bonds. Bonds with 7 percent yields, noted Rosenberg, are bargains.

Few investors wanted to own government bonds in 1997 that were paying a very handsome and guaranteed rate of 7 percent, because the crowd was enamored with a stock market that was going through the roof. So many people had their eyes fixed on stocks that bonds were virtually ignored. Few wanted to own bonds, so the yields were high in order to attract buyers. Patient investors with an eye for value will often recognize bargains that escape the public. The lessons learned from that Joe Rosenberg interview on April 14, 1997, are now legendary. The stock market finally ran out of gas in 2000. By 2002 the stock market had fallen all the way back to 1997 levels. The record market highs reached in 2000 were still standing as records by the end of 2005. And what about those 7 percent bond yields that nobody seemed to want back in 1997? Well, the smart money slipped in and bought all those bonds while no one was looking. They too are gone, for now.

When it seems as though no one is interested in bonds because they are focused on whatever seems to be working at the time, you'll know it is probably a good opportunity to back up the tractor and buy a wagonload. It is during these types of periods that it makes sense to diversify your retirement portfolio with fixed income or bonds. There will likely be many wonderful opportunities to pick up high-quality bonds at bargain prices over the next 30 or 40 years. Because bonds play such an important role in your asset allocation, one should never buy bonds for the sake of owning bonds. Buy bonds strategically for the long term when the price is right and yields are high. Try to pick up 7 percent in a solid corporate bond fund if you can. While you are waiting, don't be afraid of owning cash. Cash is an excellent asset to hold whenever you are patiently waiting for the right buying opportunity. In fact, I would much prefer cash than a subscription to automatic rebalancing services that buy bonds and allocate your portfolio automatically for you. Remember to stay away from fads and products you don't understand. Don't get suckered into chasing yield. And watch your annual fees: When purchasing flagship corporate bond funds, try to stay with those funds that charge annual fees well below 1 percent. Those who invest forever need to make sure they've capitalized on every reasonable advantage offered by the market.

Four Workhorses of Money Accumulation

Once you pass the $100,000 mark, there are three—sometimes four—sources of income, depending on your personal circumstances. First, there are your salary deferrals. Second, there are dividends from your stock mutual funds. Third, interest from your corporate bond mutual funds is present. And fourth, there is the possibility that your company is making a matching or profit-sharing contribution to the 401(k) plan on your behalf. These are the four sources of income that will largely fund the accumulation of assets as you build toward your retirement goal. Once retired, you will lose your salary deferrals and any matching or company money. Deferrals and matching contributions depend on having a job. In retirement, you are on your own. Interest and dividends will carry you the rest of the way home.

To capture a firsthand glance at how these four workhorses operate, let's take a look at an example. A worker earns $45,000 annually and has $300,000 in her 401(k) account at work. Her goal at retirement is $1,000,000. By following the bond allocation model, she has 30 percent, or $90,000, invested in a corporate bond account paying 7 percent annually, and the remaining 70 percent, or $210,000, invested in a large cap flagship mutual fund. The large cap flagship fund will pay 2 percent yearly in dividends. She is saving 20 percent of her income, or $9,000 a year. Her company is making a 3 percent matching contribution on her behalf, which totals $1,350 annually.

Each month our worker is therefore investing $750 from her payroll deferrals, $112 from her employer match, $525 from her bond interest, and $350 from dividends. Altogether she is saving $1,737 each month, or $20,844 each year. All the savings, including her bond interest, are being invested in the flagship stock fund. Incidentally, this point is exceedingly important: The cash from these four workhorses—bond interest, dividends, salary deferrals, and any company contributions—are plowed back into the stock funds. Stocks are the growth engines of wealth creation.

The sum of all her savings from these four different workhorses equals 46 percent of her annual pay. Thanks to the bond interest and stock dividends, the total amount of savings is almost equal to half of her gross wages. Should the flagship stock fund achieve an average annual return of 7.2 percent, this investor will reach $500,000 (or a half million) in about six years. Once she achieves this milestone, the half-million-dollar mark, she'll likely get to $1 million in about 8 years, provided her investments continue to earn 7 percent annually. Remarkably, her account will be growing on average by about $100,000 every two years as she progresses from $500,000 to $1 million. In other words, for every dollar our hypothetical investor saves in this illustration during the final years of wealth creation, the investment returns match the savings dollars at a rate better than 4:1.

One must first get to $100,000 before $1 million can be achieved. The process of wealth creation is defined by stages. The first stage is what Charlie Munger deems the most difficult. It is going from a net worth of zero to $100,000. I like to think of this as "getting out of the box." It is the task of building seed money. Investors must do everything in their power to save as much as possible when they are in the box. For Warren Buffett, it meant peddling 600,000 newspapers; for Charlie Munger it meant driving a yellow jalopy; for Benjamin Franklin, who had no wages, it required becoming a vegetarian. Save like crazy, even if it means getting a second job, and then master the five guiding principles of 401(k) investing. Most people must know a few things about investing once they reach the first $100,000; otherwise, they could someday fall behind.

The second stage takes one from $100,000 to his or her financial goal at retirement. This part of the journey becomes a bit easier because there are three, if not four, workhorses out in front. Here one must grab the reins and steer the wagon forward by continuing to save each pay period and allocating the portfolio between stock and bond funds. The key here is to remain in the middle of the road and stay away from the perils of fear and greed. Focus on the goal ahead, buy bonds when the price is right, load up on stocks when others are lined up at the exits, and keep the steady partners of discipline and patience nearby, always.

CHAPTER 15

Crossing the Rubicon

Let the dice fly high.
Menander, Ancient Playwright

No Turning Back

One of the more challenging investment decisions to be made by individuals takes place when they leave their jobs with a check in hand that represents their life savings. Everything they have worked toward and saved over the last 45 years is printed on a single piece of paper that is four inches wide and eight-and-one-half inches long. Where that check gets deposited and how it gets invested will largely determine the quality of one's remaining days. Should a newly minted retiree put the whole thing into the stock market and the market sells off by 25 percent within the first year, that person may very likely never recover. A new worker just starting out in the workforce will not even notice a precipitous market drop of 25 percent, but for an older retiree trying to live off the market in year 1 of retirement, such a fate could very likely spell ruin. Some have said that the first couple of years before retirement and the first two years following retirement are the most dangerous times to invest. One thing is for sure; once the check bearing one's life savings is cashed, there is no turning back on that decision.

Earlier it was stated that there are four stages of wealth creation. The first stage focuses on increasing the retirement assets on one's personal balance sheet. It is called "getting out of the box," meaning one should try to save as much as possible in order to get to $100,000 as soon as possible. Those who are "in the box," meaning their assets are under the $100,000 mark, should master the five guiding principles of 401(k) investing as well.

The second stage takes investors from $100,000 all the way to their retirement goal. Again, the focus is on building the retirement assets on their personal balance sheet. When in the second stage of wealth creation, investors must continue saving, apply the five guiding principles of 401(k) investing, and practice asset allocation. One must balance building wealth with protecting hard-earned assets when in the second stage.

The final two stages of wealth creation focus on the personal income statement. Once financial independence is achieved, investors must now generate enough income from their retirement nest egg to maintain their standard of living for as long as they remain alive. The emphasis in the final stages clearly rotates around income. The key now is to live on income without burning through principal. Additionally, one's investments must keep pace with inflation.

The third stage of wealth creation is when the income from your portfolio gets "turned on" to replace your paychecks. The specific investments made in concert with your final departure from work, in other words, are what define the third stage of wealth creation. Those unable to navigate the third stage of wealth creation can literally ruin their retirement years. Because the third stage of wealth creation coincides with the termination of your employment, mistakes can be very costly. This is what is meant by "no turning back." Once the money gets invested in Stage Three, it is difficult to turn back.

The fourth and final stage of wealth creation wholly depends on the first three stages. The fourth stage involves sitting back and living off the income from your investments that were built over a working lifetime. Those who succeed in achieving Stages One, Two, and Three will find Stage Four to be a breeze. The emphasis in Stage Four is fairly fundamental. It is all about the personal income statement. The key is to keep the cash coming in at a rate sufficient to maintain one's standard of living without diminishing one's balance sheet. Stage Four is the culmination of starting now, saving sufficient sums, and investing wisely. These are the golden years. These four stages are summarized in Figure 15-1.

FIGURE 15-1 *Four Stages of Financial Independence*

Stage One: Out of the Box

    Focus   Build personal balance sheet
    Goal   Go from zero net worth to $100,000
    Tasks   Save aggressively
             Master five guiding principles of 401(k) investing

Stage Two: Achieve Retirement Goal

    Focus   Build personal balance sheet
    Goal   Go from $100,000 to retirement goal
    Tasks   Save aggressively
             Apply five guiding principles of 401(k) investing
             Apply asset allocation

Stage Three: Execute Retirement Portfolio

    Focus   Activate personal income statement
    Goal   Create a portfolio capable of generating income to maintain
             standard of living
    Tasks   Apply asset allocation to generate monthly income and protect
             against inflation

Stage Four: Replace Earned Income with Retirement Income

    Focus   Personal income statement
    Goal   Maintain standard of living
    Tasks   Enjoy rewards of retirement

Alea iacta est: Let the Dice Fly High

There are two ways to interpret the phrase "Let the dice fly high," the literal and the allegorical. For instance, say a retirement check representing all the money someone has saved and earned over a working lifetime gets invested in the market. Because we know that no one can know for sure what the market will do tomorrow or the next day or the next year, the retirement check's owner might exclaim, "Let the dice fly high." This could represent a literal interpretation of these famous words first written by Greek playwright Menander and put to such famous use by Julius Caesar. The retirement money has been invested in one fell swoop, and the assets are now in the hands of fate. "Let the dice fly high," when used literally, implies, "Oh boy, I sure hope this works out for the best. This sure is an awfully big step." It means that person is at the mercy of the dice or largely dependent upon chance.

Then there is the allegorical. Here a person has been planning for years as to how this money should be invested since the first day of employment. The five guiding principles of 401(k) investing were taken very seriously on day 1. In other words, even though this person was starting from a net worth of zero, she was investing as though she already possessed significant sums. She faithfully plowed money into a large cap mutual fund that had been around for years. It was the flagship fund in the mutual fund family she was using. Once she crossed the $100,000 mark, she began looking to diversify into a bellwether corporate bond fund. She patiently waited for the markets to come to her with the right price. She insisted on receiving a 7 percent yield on fixed-income securities. Her asset allocation was also disciplined. She continued to carefully buy more bonds whenever prices were favorable, as her retirement balance sheet increased in value and grew closer to her goal. Finally, after nearly 40 years of working, saving, and investing, she arrived at her stated retirement goal. She was now ready to convert the income from her portfolio and replace the paychecks from her job. Following the retirement party on her last day at work, she grinned and exclaimed to her very best friends these Latin words: *Alea iacta est,* which means "let the dice fly high!" Like Caesar crossing the Rubicon, she had done everything in her power throughout her adult life to prepare for this important moment. She knew well that although she could not know what the markets would do in the next day or week or year, her lifetime of strategic planning had certainly placed her future destiny above mere chance.

The time to figure out what to do with a large check at retirement is not at age 67 or the date when one retires, but rather on the day a person begins saving and investing with a specific goal in mind. It does not matter whether someone is 10 years old or 20, 30, or 40 years old. What matters most is the goal. For example, everything about the four stages of wealth creation boils down to the financial goal at retirement. Once someone knows the dollar amount he or she must shoot for at retirement, then that person can measure progress, define what must be saved now from each paycheck, determine asset allocation, figure out how to catch up if in their 40s or 50s, and determine how that nest egg should be invested by retirement. The thread that runs so true through-out the whole process of individual wealth creation, from start to finish, is the goal found in Figure 5-1, which defines the amount of money one must have at retirement. People who become wealthy know their goal. Their retirement goal is just as tangible as was Rome for Caesar. Caesar knew exactly where he wanted to end up in life. Those who save and in-vest seriously for retirement know also where they want to end up. This is the secret, if there is such a thing, to financial independence. People who become wealthy can pinpoint their financial destination in life.

The final check at retirement should really not be a big deal. It ide-ally has already been taken care of years and years before. The nest egg at retirement is nothing more than a continuum of that which is already in place. There are fixed-income investments able to spin off enough in cash to meet one's current standard of living. The rest is all in stocks. The stocks protect the portfolio from the hazards of inflation. As the cost of living increases, which it surely will over time, all one has to do is simply transfer money from stocks over to bonds to pick up a pay in-crease. A ratio of 70 percent fixed income to 30 percent stocks should serve most who have reached their goal at retirement well, especially if the fixed income is yielding somewhere around 7 percent.

Final Thoughts

A 10-year-old boy asked the world's greatest investor how one should save and make money. It is a question that all who participate in 401(k)s should be able to answer. It starts, as we now know, with a goal. A 10-year-old who wishes to become a millionaire by retirement needs to have $20,000 already put away and invested. A 10-year-old who does not have $20,000, but still wants to retire with $1 million, can still get there by sav-ing roughly $100 a month. A 20-year-old with the same goal, needs to have $40,000 invested. Should a 20-year-old lack $40,000, he can get to $1 million by saving around $212 a month for the next 47 years. The key to saving and investing is familiarity with one's ultimate financial goal.

Those who are working and wanting to someday retire must calcu-late the value of their jobs in future dollars. That, as we learned earlier, is also the definition of financial independence. It is the point behind saving and investing. The process of wealth creation, exemplified by the four stages of financial independence, is coming up with the means to replace your job. Explaining to someone how one replaces his or her job is the same thing as telling someone how to become wealthy.

The process, as demonstrated by Benjamin Franklin, is democratic. Anyone can travel successfully from zero net worth to financial independence. Those who earn less will have to paddle harder, but they can still achieve success. Franklin demonstrated that important lesson also.

Contrary to conventional thought, one does not have to be smarter than the average guy, get better investment returns than the average guy, or make more money than the average guy. In fact, one can even be slightly below average on all three of those scores and still wind up just fine. The achievement of wealth, remember always, is doggedly democratic. Wealth rewards discipline, patience, and determination. It is a self-controlled process. That means each person individually runs the show.

Bonnie and I started out on the wealth-creation road in May of 1985. We crossed the finish line in 2004 when I retired and came home. There is nothing extraordinary about our backgrounds or college educations. Bonnie earned a degree in nursing; mine was in liberal arts. We did, however, make it a practice to always save as much as possible. Looking back, we don't ever recall saving less than 20 percent of our gross wages—and there were some years when we put away more.

Early on in the wealth-creation process, it often is very difficult for people to imagine what it would be like to have several hundred thousand dollars. That is a common symptom of "being in the box." It is when you work and scrape to get ahead by, let's say, $15,000. But $15,000 seems so very far away from $500,000. The distance between Point A ($15,000) and Point B ($500,000) seems unfathomable.

It is at these critical junctures that you must not allow yourself to think you are an exception to the rule. The three constants—start now, save sufficient sums, and invest wisely—worked for Benjamin Franklin, Warren Buffett, and Charlie Munger, and they will work for you, just as these same three rules have worked for literally millions who once were in your exact same shoes. The road to wealth is a well-trodden path. So, whenever you start to doubt the rules, grit your teeth and stay with the program until you reach $100,000 and get out of the box. The one lesson I can share with absolute conviction, based on my own experiences, is that once you achieve six figures in savings, the path ahead becomes clearer and the end more believable.

Let me add also that the road to financial independence is not all gloomy and austere. Brightness and fun are not comprised of stuff. Benjamin Franklin had a marvelous and enduring sense of humor. Many of his practical jokes are still legendary. Likewise, Buffett and Munger often display a wonderful sense of humor and lightheartedness when appearing publicly. When individuals take the time to reflect on those moments that have brought them great joy, happiness, and satisfaction, material stuff and things are usually noticeably missing. It is erroneous to think under spending brings misery and deprivation. The absence of financial worry goes a long way toward the creation of a light heart.

Money is not without limitations. It cannot replace lost time, it cannot buy friendship, and it cannot compensate for poor health. There are, in my judgment, many things more valuable than money. The rich cannot buy a more brilliant sunrise, a warmer fire, or friendlier puppies. Wealth is considerably inferior to honor, virtue, or valor. Those who place too much value on money risk living empty lives.

Money is best understood as being utilitarian. It buys food, shelter, clothing, and sometimes provides mortals with a certain measure of independence and dignity. That basically is why we work. Americans are now confronted with the challenges of an emerging ownership society. Ownership means many things, but, for workers, ownership will soon mean individuals must replace their jobs with financial independence if they ever hope to retire. This enchiridion on wealth and its creation is offered to these workers as an answer to these times.

Notes

Epigraph

1. Peter L. Bernstein, *Against the Gods,* (New York: John Wiley & Sons, Inc., 1996), p. 15.

Introduction

1. Effective in 2006, 401(k) plans were permitted to adopt special Roth provisions. These changes allow for after-tax payroll contributions wherein earnings can potentially grow tax free.

Chapter 1 The Reckoning

1. Used by permission of the estate of Robert Service, c/o M. Wm. Krasilovsky.

2. Peter Thiel, "Game Theory," Interview with Eric Savitz, *Barrons,* March 1, 2004, pp. F 3–4.

3. Peter Orszag, "Balances in Defined Contribution Plans and IRAs," *Urban Institute,* Tax Analysis, February 2, 2004, p. 1.

4. Peter L. Bernstein, *The Power of Gold* (New York: John Wiley & Sons, 2000), p. 227.

5. William Manchester, *The Glory and the Dream* (New York: Bantam, 1974), p. 148.

6. Doris Kearns Goodwin, *No Ordinary Time* (New York: Touchstone, 1994), p. 513.

7. James Bond Stockdale, *Thoughts of a Philosophical Fighter Pilot* (Stanford: Hoover Institution Press, 1995), p. 185.

8. Michael Knox Beran, *Jefferson's Demons* (New York: Free Press, 2003), p. 71.

Chapter 2 The Oracle

1. Janet Lowe, *Damn Right! Behind the Scenes with Berkshire Hathaway Billionaire Charlie Munger* (New York: John Wiley & Sons, 2000), p. 136. The Charlie Munger quotes reused from *Damn Right!* are reprinted with permission of John Wiley & Sons, Inc.

2. Warren Buffett and Charlie Munger, "What Makes the Investment Game Great Is You Don't Have to Be Right on *Everything*," *Outstanding Investor Digest,* Vol. XVIII, Nos. 3 & 4 (Year-end 2003 ed.), p. 1.

3. Roger Lowenstein, *Buffett: The Making of an American Capitalist* (New York: Random House, 1995), p. 162.

4. Lowe, *Damn Right!,* p. iii.

5. Warren Buffett and Charlie Munger: "The Incentives in Hedge Funds Are Awesome, But Don't Expect The Returns to Be Too Swift," *Outstanding Investor Digest,* Vol. XVI, Nos. 4 & 5 (Year-end 2001 ed.), p. 43.

6. Carlos Baker, *Emerson Among the Eccentrics* (New York: Viking, 1996), p. 104.

7. Carole Loomis and Warren Buffett, "Mr. Buffett on the Stock Market," *Fortune,* Vol. 140, No. 10, Special Issue. (November 22, 1999).

8. Lowenstein, *Buffett,* p. 34.

9. Buffett and Munger, "The Incentives in Hedge Funds Are Awesome," p. 44.

10. Lowenstein, *Buffett,* p. 33.

11. Warren Buffett, "The Best Advice I Ever Got," *Fortune*, Vol. 151, No. 6 (March 21, 2005), p. 92.

12. Lowenstein, *Buffett*, p. 20.

13. Jason Zweig, "What Warren Buffett Wants You to Know," *CNN/ Money Magazine*, May 3, 2004. Retrieved from *www.money.cnn.com* 5/3/ 04.

14. Lowenstein, *Buffett*, p. 62.

15. Lowe, *Damn Right!*, p. 2.

16. Ibid, p. 35.

17. Ibid, p. 39.

18. Ibid, p. 41.

19. Ibid, p. 43.

20. Ibid, p. 45.

21. Ibid, p. 42.

22. Warren Buffett, "Warren Buffett on the Stock Market," *Fortune*, "Investors Guide 2002," December 10, 2001, p. 85.

23. Buffett and Munger, "What Makes the Investment Game Great," p. 52.

24. Lowe, *Damn Right!*, p. 54.

25. Warren Buffett and Charlie Munger, "We Use the Phrase 'Wretched Excess' Because These Are Wretched Consequences," *Outstanding Investor Digest*, Vol. XV, Nos. 3 & 4 (December 18, 2000), p. 60.

26. Samuel Eliot Morison, Henry Steele Commager, and William Leuchtenberg, *The Growth of the American Republic*, 6th ed., Vol. 1 (New York: Oxford University Press, 1969), p. 111.

27. H. W. Brands, *The First American: The Life and Times of Benjamin Franklin* (New York: Doubleday, 2000), p. 6.

28. Charlie Munger, "Shareholder Democracy? That's a Fiction. And Analysts Were *Always* Shills to Some Degree," *Outstanding Investor Digest*, Vol. XVII, Nos. 3 & 4, (December 31, 2002), p. 35.

29. L. Jesse Lemisch, ed., *Benjamin Franklin: The Autobiography and Other Writings* (New York: Signet, 1961), p. 35.

30. Ibid, p. 182.

31. Lowe, *Damn Right!*, p. 267.

Chapter 3 Three Constants of Wealth Creation

1. *BusinessWeek,* July 18, 2005, p.16.

2. Steven F. Venti and David A. Wise, "Choice, Chance, and Wealth Dispersion at Retirement," Working Paper 7521, National Bureau of Economic Research, Cambridge, Massachusetts, February 2000, p. 34.

3. Ibid, p. 35.

4. Benjamin Franklin, *The Way to Wealth* (Bedford: Applewood, 1986), p. 19.

5. Charles D. Ellis, *Winning the Loser's Game* (New York: McGraw-Hill, 1998), p. 5.

6. Jeremy T. Siegel, *Stocks for the Long Run* (New York: McGraw-Hill, 2002), p. 360.

7. Jonathan Fuerbringer, "Why Both Bulls and Bears Can Act So Bird-Brained," *New York Times,* March 31, 1997, Section 3, p. 1.

8. Ellis, *Winning the Loser's Game,* p. 29.

9. Andy Serwer, "Warren Buffett, The Oracle of Everything," retrieved 8 April 2003 from *www.fortune.com.*

10. William Shakespeare, "Julius Caesar," *The Tragedies Vol. III* (Hertfordshire, U.K.: Wordsworth Editions, Ltd., 2002), p. 64.

Chapter 4 The First Million Dollars

1. Lemisch, ed., p. 185.

2. Berkshire Hathaway, Inc., *1996 Annual Report,* p. 17.

3. $10,000 is rounded from $10,167.

4. These figures are net of fees.

Chapter 5 Setting a Personal Retirement Goal: Steps 1 and 2

1. The formula for Figure 5-1 is as follows: $0.8 \times 20 \times (1.02)^n$. A person will need 20 times her current income at retirement. The given target at retirement is adjusted for an annual 2 percent increase in

inflation. After adjusting for inflation, to maintain her standard of living this person will need only 80 percent of her target because, once retired, she is no longer deferring into the 401(k).

$$n = \text{years to retirement}$$

One can adjust the inflation factor by changing 1.02. For example, if one prefers a 4 percent inflation factor, 1.02 becomes 1.04.

2. Tennessee Williams, *Cat on a Hot Tin Roof* (New York: New Directions Publishing, 2004), p. 55.

3. The retirement goal is based on the assumption that once retired a person will refrain from depleting principal. Throughout retirement, one should expect the initial lump sum, plus any growth resulting from inflation, to remain intact since it is impossible to predict life expectancy on an individual, case by case basis.

4. Readers are sometimes curious about the impact of taxes on retirement income. Money withdrawn from a 401(k) or IRA rollover is taxed as ordinary income. As life expectancy decreases, required minimum distributions will eventually exceed 5 percent of one's account balance. Assuming one is living comfortably on 5 percent annual distributions, any required minimum distribution in excess of 5 percent will require older retirees to prepay IRS obligations.

Fortunately, there is some relief in offsets. Money outside an IRA qualifies for favorable capital gains, as well as a qualified dividend treatment when applicable. The bottom line is this: As one grows older in retirement, it is unlikely that taxes will negatively impact a person's standard of living. Taxes and birthdays in retirement are generally good things. The alternatives are what get investors!

Chapter 6 Measuring Savings Progress:
Steps 3 and 4

1. Richard P. Feynman, *Surely You're Joking Mr. Feynman* (New York: W.H. Norton, 1985), p. 343.

2. The formula for Figure 6-1, Column A is $1 \div (1.072)^n$.

$$n = \text{years}$$

To change the annual rate of return from 7.2 percent, the formula can be adjusted in the following manner. For example, a 6 percent annual rate of return reads $1 \div (1.06)^n$.

3. Drawing from the form and structure of money growth as outlined in Chapter 4, $81,800 represents the amount of money this hypothetical 31-year-old needs to attain a goal of $1,000,090 at age 67 without ever again saving. This is what it means to be on track. In other words, $81,800 compounding at 7.2 percent will equal $1,000,090 after 36 years.

Chapter 7 The Final Step: Step 5

1. MetLife Mature Market Institute, "Boomers Worried about Retirement Funds," *Plansponsor.com*, October 13, 2005, *www.plansponsor.com*.

2. Joakim Garff, trans. Bruce H. Kirmmse, *Soren Kierkegaard* (Princeton, NJ: Princeton University Press, 2005), p. 58.

Chapter 8 The Early Saving Years

1. Janet Lowe, *Damn Right! Behind the Scenes with Berkshire Hathaway Billionaire Charlie Munger* (New York: John Wiley & Sons, 2000), p. 242.

2. Thomas J. Stanley and William D. Danko, *The Millionaire Next Door* (Marietta, GA: Longstreet Press, 1996.), p. 16.

Chapter 9 Catching Up on Retirement Savings in Your 40s and 50s

1. Daniel Defoe, *Robinson Crusoe* (New York: Fine Creative Media, 2003), p. 137.

2. $0.00417 = (0.05 \div 12)$ rounded.

3. The formula for Figure 9-1 is $(1.072)^n$.

Chapter 10 A Mind for Investing

1. Berkshire Hathaway, Inc., *1996 Annual Report*, p. 17.

2. Peter Lynch, *Peter Lynch Market Commentary*, Fidelity Investments, September 20, 2001.

3. Hersh Shefrin, *Beyond Fear and Greed* (Boston: Harvard Business School Press, 2000), p. 24.

4. Charles D. Ellis, *Winning the Loser's Game* (New York: McGraw-Hill, 1998), p. 125.

5. Melissa Turner, "Nebraska Billionaire Has Purchased 6.3% of Coca-Cola Stock," *The Atlanta Journal*, March 16, 1989, p. A/1.

6. Robert G. Hagstrom, *The Essential Buffett* (New York: John Wiley & Sons, 2001), p. 108.

7. Andrew Kilpatrick, *Warren Buffett: The Good Guy of Wall Street* (New York: Donald I. Fine, 1992), p. 123.

8. Hagstrom, *The Essential Buffett*, p. 200.

9. Jeremy Siegel, *Stocks for the Long Run* (New York: McGraw-Hill, 2002), p. 27.

10. Mark Hubert, "Aging Brings Wisdom, But Not on Investing," *The New York Times, Sunday Money*, December 4, 2005, p. 6.

Chapter 11 Getting an Edge in the Market

1. Janet Lowe, *Damn Right! Behind the Scenes with Berkshire Hathaway Billionaire Charlie Munger* (New York: John Wiley & Sons, 2000), p. 231.

2. David McCullough, *Truman* (New York: Simon & Schuster, 1992), p. 66.

3. Janet Lowe, *The Man Who Beats the S&P: Investing with Bill Miller* (New York: John Wiley & Sons, 2002), p. 161.

4. David McCullough, *Truman*, p. 67.

5. Charles Ellis, *Winning the Loser's Game* (New York: McGraw-Hill, 1998), p. 56.

6. John Train, *The Money Masters* (New York: Harper & Row, 1980), p. 158.

7. Lowe, *Damn Right!*, p. 225.

8. Robert Lenzner and David S. Fondiller, "The Not-So-Silent Partner," *Forbes*, January 22, 1996, p. 80.

Chapter 12 The Irony of Making Money

1. Ralph Wanger, *A Zebra in Lion Country* (New York: Simon & Schuster, 1997), p. 173.

2. Warren Buffett, "Warren Buffett on the Stock Market," *Fortune,* December 10, 2001, p. 88.

Chapter 13 Retirement Investments

1. Jeffrey Archer, *Kane & Abel* (New York: Simon & Schuster, 1979), p. 69.

2. Jeremy J. Siegel, *The Future for Investors* (New York: Crown Business, 2005), p. 13.

3. The point to Marlboro Friday is that income-producing investments tend to give investors distinct advantages whenever the income is reinvested into those same shares at lower prices. The case of Philip Morris (Altria) is unique in that it involved a single security. Looking back in time we can see the positive impact of this particular story. Looking forward, however, investors must understand that it is preferable to hold investments that are diversified mutual funds wherein the income produced by these funds is reinvested into equity mutual funds that have a negligible probability of ever falling all the way to zero in price.

4. Op cit., p. 142.

5. Ibid.

6. Ibid.

7. Ibid

Chapter 14 Managing Your Retirement Portfolio

1. Warren Buffett and Charlie Munger, "Asset Allocation Is Pure Nonsense. The Best Way to Minimize Risk Is to *Think,*" *Outstanding Investor Digest,* Vol. XIX, Nos. 3 & 4 (December 31, 2004), p. 40.

2. Kathryn Welling, "There Are Alternatives: A Seasoned Pro, Wary of Greed, Steers Clear of the Crowd." *Barrons,* April 14, 1977.

Index